FRENCH THOUGHT
SINCE 1600

FRENCH THOUGHT
SINCE 1600

D. C. Potts
and
D. G. Charlton

Revised and reprinted
from
France: A Companion to French Studies
EDITED BY D. G. CHARLTON

METHUEN

FRANCE: A COMPANION TO FRENCH STUDIES
first published in 1972
by Methuen & Co Ltd
11 New Fetter Lane London EC4
Printed in Great Britain
by Richard Clay (The Chaucer Press), Ltd
Bungay, Suffolk
These chapters, revised and expanded, first published as a
University Paperback in 1974
This edition © 1974 Methuen & Co Ltd

ISBN 0 416 81630 4

Distributed in the USA by
HARPER & ROW PUBLISHERS INC.
BARNES & NOBLE IMPORT DIVISION

CONTENTS

EDITOR'S PREFACE

The chapters in this volume first appeared in *France: A Companion to French Studies* in 1972 (London, Methuen, x + 613 pp.). That work – ranging over French history and society, thought, literature, painting, sculpture and architecture, music, and politics and institutions from the Renaissance to the present – is inevitably lengthy and proportionately costly. It has thus been suggested that particular chapters which together provide a very useful treatment of their subject should be made available in cheaper format. That is the aim of the series to which this book belongs, covering respectively:

1 *French History and Society: The Wars of Religion to the Fifth Republic*
   (Dr Roger Mettam and Professor Douglas Johnson)
2 *French Thought since 1600*
   (Dr D. C. Potts and Professor D. G. Charlton)
3 *French Literature from 1600 to the Present*
   (Professor W. D. Howarth, Professor Henri M. Peyre and Professor John Cruickshank)
4 *French Art and Music since 1500*
   (Professor Sir Anthony Blunt and the late Mr Edward Lockspeiser)
   (with illustrations not included in the original volume)
5 *Contemporary France: Politics, Society and Institutions*
   (Professor Jean Blondel, in an expanded treatment of his subject)

Each study has been revised, with additional material where necessary, and the original brief bibliographies have been expanded into the form of bibliographical essays. Given 'the chastening insight [in Professor Sir Ernst Gombrich's words] that no culture can be mapped out in its entirety, but no element of this culture can be understood in isolation', one may regret that these chapters should be torn from their original context, and it is greatly to be hoped that those interested in individual elements of French culture will refer to the total volume to complete their understanding. Yet it is the Editor's belief, even so, that this present book provides, at a price which most would-be purchasers can afford, an informative, up-to-date guide and evaluation.

D. G. CHARLTON

Department of French Studies
University of Warwick
February 1974

FRENCH THOUGHT IN THE SEVENTEENTH AND EIGHTEENTH CENTURIES

D. C. Potts

The Seventeenth Century

If one were required to sum up the history of French thought in the seventeenth and eighteenth centuries in a single statement, it would be that this was the epoch which saw the rise of rationalist philosophy and liberal ideology. In the movement to free the human mind from the tyranny of traditional authority which characterizes this period in European thought as a whole, French thinkers played a prominent part, and by the end of the eighteenth century they were the intellectual leaders of Europe, having upheld the ideals of democratic government, humanitarian ethics and religious toleration, and having adumbrated in their philosophical thought the evolutionary materialism of the nineteenth century. These notions were developed gradually, through a series of shifts of emphasis, so that any chronological division of the period is bound to be arbitrary; but for expository purposes it is convenient to think of it as falling into three parts. The mechanistic view of the world which is the main feature of seventeenth-century thought had effectively supplanted traditional scholastic philosophy (though this continued to be taught in schools and universities) by the 1670s; on the other hand, the evolutionary materialism which is the most striking feature in the eighteenth century did not achieve coherent expression until the 1750s. This leaves us with an intermediate period, between 1670 and 1750, in which scientific and metaphysical issues, although still important, take second place to the use of reason as a weapon of criticism aimed not only at ideas but at religious, moral and political institutions, which constitutes what is perhaps the best-known aspect of the eighteenth-century 'Enlightenment'.

It is in the first half of the seventeenth century that reason (which on close inspection turns out to be a protean term) ceases to be subordinated to the authority of tradition, and comes to replace tradition as a means of knowledge and a guide to life. Rationalism in this sense is particularly associated with the rise of modern science. Galileo and Kepler, basing themselves on Copernicus's heliocentric theory, described the universe as a machine, operating according to laws which could be expressed as mathematical formulae. Mechanism was taken up in France by the philosophers and scientists (the seventeenth and eighteenth centuries recognized no real distinction between the two categories) in the circle of the Minorite Father Marin Mersenne (1588–1648). Mersenne's circle set an early example of co-operative scientific endeavour, which eventually gave rise to the founding of the officially sponsored Académie des Sciences in 1669. Among the best-known members of Mersenne's original group were Pierre Gassendi[1] (1592–1655) and René Descartes (1596–1650). The chief obstacles to their attempts to establish the mechanistic interpretation of nature in France were the widespread diffusion of scepticism and the authority of Aristotelianism. Scepticism had been given a powerful impetus towards the end of the sixteenth century by Montaigne's *Apologie de Raimond de Sebond*: Montaigne's contention that the mind is inherently incapable of attaining truth because of its dependence on the senses was extremely influential in the early part of the seventeenth century, partly (as will be seen) on account of the support it was believed to give to a certain type of religious apologetics. Mersenne and Gassendi countered this with what has been termed a 'mitigated scepticism': Mersenne, in particular, argued that men possess a principle of reflection which is independent of the senses.

Scepticism threatened the belief that *any* valid science could be established. Aristotelianism, on the other hand, specifically stood in the way of the establishment of the mechanistic science of Galileo and Kepler. Aristotle's philosophy had given rise to two quite different scientific doctrines. The scholastic science taught in France was an amalgam of Christian theology with Aristotle's physics. It taught that the earth was at the centre of the universe, and that round it moved the spheres which carried the sun, the moon and the remaining planets. Although the privileged position occupied by the earth showed that man was a unique creature, destined by God for salvation, man's fall from grace, recorded in the Bible, had made the region 'below' the moon into one

[1] Gassendi's influence was restricted by the fact that he wrote only in Latin. A French digest of his philosophy began to appear only in the 1670s.

of change and decay, whereas that 'above' the moon was unchanging
and the abode of the angels. Everything in nature had its proper 'place',
assigned to it by God, to which it tended to move. Beyond what was
immediately explicable in terms of the 'qualities' (hot, dry, moist, cold)
apprehended by the senses, movement took place as the result of an
'occult' (or secret) quality placed in objects by God – thus the magnet
was held to attract by virtue of an inherent 'attractive quality'. One of
the major achievements of the new science was to get rid of such purely
verbal explanations by substituting considerations of quantity for those
of quality: it dealt only with the objectively measurable features
of the shape, mass and displacement of objects, using which movement
could be expressed in mathematical terms. The French mechanists had
also to contend with naturalism, a development of Aristotle's biology,
independent of theology, which had originated in Italy at the University of Padua, and was diffused in France in the early seventeenth century by Italian visitors, notably Vanini and Campanella, and by the
French writers Théophile de Viau (1590–1626) and Cyrano de Bergerac
(1619–55). Naturalism differed from scholastic Aristotelianism in an
important respect. For the scholastics, God was the Prime Mover who
had set a universe of inert matter in motion; for the naturalists, God was
the source of a force or vital principle diffused throughout and animating all matter, and known as 'nature' or the 'world soul'. Like
scholastic science, naturalism was incompatible with an explanation of
the operations of nature based on mechanical cause and effect. Aristotelianism was under increasingly heavy fire in France in the period between 1620 and 1640, notably in Gassendi's *Exercitationes paradoxicae*
(1624). Gassendi's positive contribution, in his *Syntagma philosophicum*
(1658), was to replace the Aristotelian scheme of qualities by a revival
of classical Epicurean science, taking as the elementary data of physics
the 'atoms' (the smallest units of matter) which constantly separate and
combine to form the phenomena we observe, and which, possessing
inertia and moving in a vacuum, can be made the foundation of a
mechanical representation of nature.

Mersenne and Gassendi based their scientific theories on observation
and claimed for them only conjectural status. Descartes took an entirely
different view. He turned his back on empiricism and claimed to have
discovered the metaphysical basis on which scientific certainty could
be founded. Although his arguments were at first sharply criticized,
not least by his immediate colleagues, and although nearly every one
of his conclusions was subsequently shown to be wrong, the way in

which he seemed to have disposed once and for all of both scepticism and scholasticism, together with the broad sweep of his philosophy, in which he proposed to extend the mechanistic approach to all branches of knowledge, made a profound impression on his contemporaries and left a mark which is still visible in the philosophical discussions of our own day. An attractive account of his highly individual quest for truth, and of the outlines of his philosophy, is to be found in the *Discours de la méthode* (1637), but for a fuller understanding of his thought, and the problems to which it gave rise, it is necessary to go to his other works and especially to the *Méditations métaphysiques* (in Latin, 1642; in French, 1644). Descartes turned the sceptics' own weapon against them, and showed that the outcome of the most rigorous process of doubt was the certainty of one proposition, 'Je pense, donc je suis', on which, armed with the right criterion of truth, a whole system of positive knowledge could then be erected. Descartes discovered his criterion (confirmed in his apprehension of the truth of the *cogito* itself) in mathematics, where truth is perceived as a clear and distinct intuition, is independent of the senses, and leads to the discovery of other truths by deduction. By extending the mathematical method of discovery to all branches of knowledge, Descartes was able to carry science well beyond the stage of a collection of *ad hoc* findings based on the provisional acceptance of sense data at which Mersenne and Gassendi were prepared to leave it, but in doing so he raised problems which were to have far-reaching implications in the period with which we are concerned in this chapter, and which have continued to provoke controversy right up to our own times – in his book *The Concept of Mind*, Gilbert Ryle goes so far as to attribute all the errors of modern philosophy to Descartes.

The central problem arises out of the radical way in which Descartes distinguished between the activity of the mind, including thinking, feeling and willing, which takes place in a realm of immaterial spirit, and the mechanically determined world of material objects (including the human body) perceived by the senses. This distinction, which scholastic philosophy had mitigated by speaking of a threefold soul in man, part 'vegetative' (which man shared with the plants), part 'sensitive' (shared with the animals), and part 'rational' (unique in man among the creatures of nature), the lower parts being included in the higher, raised two difficulties in particular. In the first place, Descartes claimed that all knowledge is innate, our ideas being somehow latent in the mind, so that sense experience merely triggers them off. Although Descartes seems at first to have wanted to restrict this to the claim that certain operations of the mind are innate, he was led into the position of asserting that the ideas of God, the soul, the extended universe of matter, and many others, were present in the mind at birth. In the second place, Descartes found it difficult to account for the interaction, an undeniable fact of experience, of immaterial mind and material body. His solution was to represent the mind as what Ryle has called 'a ghost in the machine', situated according to Descartes in the pineal gland, which lies at the base of the brain. Descartes explained bodily movement as the result of the displacement of small particles of matter (traditionally but misleadingly, in his view, known as 'animal spirits') along the nerves, which he conceived as being like hollow tubes, in such a way as to provoke muscular reactions.

It is characteristic of Descartes's reliance on the operations of his own mind to reach the truth about the physical world that he made no observations to verify his theory concerning the pineal gland or the structure of the nerves. He used experiment only to give the mind something to explain, or at the most to illustrate a theory, but not to corroborate or invalidate it. Even mathematics, the basis of his thought, provided him only with a criterion of metaphysical truth and a model of logical method. Although he had invented, in analytical or 'Cartesian' geometry, the mathematical tool which (as Mersenne had seen) was needed if the chaos of appearances was to be given a rational interpretation, he rarely made use of it in his own work, preferring to deduce the structure of reality from a primary intuition.

The bias of the mechanists' efforts was utilitarian, and they concentrated on the operations of nature rather than on its ultimate cause in God. As a result, some modern critics have accused them of holding views or harbouring intentions incompatible with their professions of Christian belief. But the impact of mechanistic science on religious thought was insidious rather than dramatic. Although the new cosmology shattered the scholastic distinction between the supralunary and the sublunary regions, and displaced man from his special position at the centre of the universe to set him wandering amongst the stars in the infinity of space, this seems to have served more as a lesson of Christian humility than as a sign that God had retreated from His creation. Mechanism could conflict with the letter of Scripture, as Galileo discovered, but the French mechanists did not press the point. The empiricists amongst them were fideists: that is to say, they held that scepticism had shown up the inadequacy of all proofs of natural theology (which comprised principally the existence of God and the immortality of the soul), and that all the doctrines of Christianity should therefore be accepted on the authority of revelation alone. Although a significant departure from the doctrine of Aquinas, fideism was looked on with favour by Catholic theologians who regarded scepticism of this kind as a bulwark against both Protestant and freethinking rationalism. While it went out of favour when Cartesian rationalism gained ground in the second half of the century, fideism was not officially condemned by the Vatican until 1870. Although Descartes distinguished between the doctrines of Christianity, which are 'above reason', and the certainties of science, which are discoverable by reason, in a quasi-fideistic manner, his position was rather different from that of Mersenne or Gassendi, in that his proofs of God and the soul provided apologists with new arguments and were used to promote a revival of natural theology. The empiricists saw in the order and harmony of the universal machine support for the 'moral' proof of God's existence known as the argument from design. Descartes, by arguing from the concept of existence to the existence of an infinite and perfect Being, produced a proof which did not depend, like the argument from design, on the fallible evidence of the senses. On the question of the soul, Descartes claimed only to know that it is immaterial, but the apologists who followed in his traces found it a short step to assert its immortality. Descartes's somewhat off-handed attitude towards revealed theology, and the single-mindedness with which he applied himself to the discovery of rational certitudes and the promotion of the utilitarian aim of his philosophy, have caused doubts to be cast on his sincerity. It is clear, however, from the *Méditations* that the existence of God was vitally necessary to him. That God exists and does not deceive us (the hypothesis of the 'malin génie' which Descartes raises and refutes) is the corner-stone of his entire philosophy: without it, human certainty would be impossible.

The group of thinkers more legitimately suspect of using fideism as a cover for unbelief are the *libertins*. The French word means a freethinker, but not necessarily a person of loose morals, as does its English equivalent. A *libertin* might be an atheist, a deist, or a heterodox Christian. The most notable seventeenth-century *libertins* are those who have been called 'libertins érudits' because they believed that in so far as truth was to be found at all, it would be through learning and not through speculation. They include François La Mothe le Vayer (1588–1672), Gabriel Naudé (1600–53) and Gui Patin (1601–72), all of whom were friends of Gassendi, who shared some of their views. They were sceptics, but they were influenced by Italian rationalism as well as by Montaigne. Following the Paduan philosopher Pomponazzi, they did not look upon faith and reason as two ways to religious truth, but as attitudes attributable to two classes of men, the philosophers who use reason to become 'déniaisés' and to lead a moral life in which virtue is practised for its own sake and not out of fear of hell-fire or hope of future rewards; and the masses, the slaves of ignorance and passions, who need religious belief and institutions to provide them with laws of conduct. They did not believe in enlightening the masses, and so conformed outwardly to established beliefs and customs while reserving the right to draw their own private conclusions. These were often provocative, even though habitually approached through the study of pagan religion, the inference being left open that Christianity did not constitute a special case. They propagated the view that religious institutions are not divine in origin, but are 'useful inventions' of politicians for their own ends. They were inclined to regard these ends as good and believed that religious uniformity was a prerequisite of political stability; as a result, they were unsympathetic to the idea of religious toleration. The same theory could, however, be developed into a denunciation of religions as 'impostures', and the legend that the world's great religions had been founded by three impostors, Moses, Christ and Mahomet, goes back to this period, although it reached the height of its diffusion in the clandestine manuscript literature of the early eighteenth century. The *libertins* expressed other views which tended to conflict with contemporary Christianity. If Patin stopped short at a vociferous anticlericalism, La Mothe le Vayer formulated a catalogue of doubts so universal as to undermine the current fideistic doctrine (which he claimed to espouse) that scepticism is essentially a Christian philosophy, while Naudé used doubt more systematically to criticize the content of the classical myths in a way which also seemed to call belief in the Christian supernatural into question.

The *libertin* belief that, for the enlightened élite, virtue is its own reward, is an indication that an element of rationalism is to be found in seventeenth-century ethical thought independently of the impact of science which, in this field, directly influenced only the moral ideas of Descartes (who linked morality with an understanding of the body as a machine) and perhaps of Gassendi (since Epicurean ethics was based on the physics). It is essentially a Stoic notion, and both Stoic and

Epicurean ideas appealed to contemporary Frenchmen, many of whom saw moral problems in terms of the capriciousness of fortune in the uncertain times leading up to the civil war of the Frondes (1649–53). Seventeenth-century 'Stoicism' and 'Epicureanism' are overlapping categories. Few adepts of the former preached the full rigour of the doctrine that the sage must be impassive, while few of Epicurus' seventeenth-century disciples gave themselves up wholly to sensual debauchery: the serious moralists of both persuasions took the view that, as Edgar Wind has put it, virtue ought not to be deficient in pleasure, nor pleasure in virtue. Nevertheless, the distinction between them is a useful one, particularly when we consider the relationship of pagan moral ideas to Christianity in this period. Gassendi, who rehabilitated Epicurus' physics, also rehabilitated his ethics, the basis of which is the empirical observation that it is a law of nature that we should seek pleasure and avoid pain. But Epicurus specified as the major obstacle to pleasure our fear that the gods may harm us, in this world or in an after-life. He therefore set out to prove scientifically that the gods have no interest in human affairs, and that the soul does not survive the death of the body. Gassendi, on the other hand, performed the *tour de force* of reversing Epicurus' argument and claiming that it is Christianity, with its assurance of a benevolent God and its promise of eternal bliss, that is the best remover of fear. Gassendi thus provided those of his contemporaries, who were otherwise indifferent to religion, with an ulterior motive for seeking to be convinced of its truth. A case in point is that of Saint-Évremond (1614–1703), whom we shall meet again in another connection; Saint-Évremond was a disciple of Gassendi who for a time looked for religious certainty in fideistic acceptance and in Cartesian demonstrations, but he also differed significantly from his master in stressing the importance of the passions as a principle of action, and his own brand of Epicureanism comes as close as any French thinker's to that of Hobbes, whose definition of life as a 'continual process of striving and desiring' Saint-Évremond seems to echo.

The accommodation of Stoic ideas to Christian moral teaching had taken place long before the seventeenth century. Theologians had incorporated into the Christian doctrine of the Fall, as a result of which reason became a source of error and the passions, attracting the will, a cause of sin, the Stoic notion that a principle of 'right reason' and a knowledge of natural law have been implanted in all men, thus making virtuous action possible despite the ravages of original sin. This point of view dominates the many moral treatises of the first part of the seventeenth century which it is convenient to range under the banner of 'Christian Stoicism', the most noteworthy example being the Oratorian Senault's *De l'usage des passions* (1641). But Anthony Levi, in an essential book, has shown how 'right reason', which originally included both intuitive intellect and moral will, and enabled a man to control his passions in accordance with God's purposes, was already split up into 'reason', narrowed down to its analytical and critical functions, and will, considered as an autonomous faculty which puts the promptings of reason into action. Reason thus becomes the faculty which makes calculations of self-interest rather than the faculty (akin to conscience) which has an intuitive apprehension of God's will. This development reached its culmination in Descartes's *Les Passions de l'âme* (1649), a work which gives us a sufficient clue to the nature of the definitive ethical treatise which Descartes projected as the crown of his philosophy, but did not live to write. It is clear that Descartes considered ethics to depend on scientific knowledge of the union of the spiritual soul with the mechanism of the body. His ideal is the *généreux* who resolves to use rational judgement and autonomous will to manipulate his passions in such a way as to exercise complete control over his actions. For the passions are neither good nor bad in themselves, but are disturbances of the soul caused by the displacement of the animal spirits as the result of some external stimulus, which we can counter by switching the spirits in the pineal gland into some other part of the body. Descartes's theory of the passions is an outstanding example of the extreme point reached by optimistic ethical humanism in the seventeenth century. His moral ideal bears a superficial resemblance to that of Corneille's stage heroes, but in the cult of glory which affected large numbers of the French nobility in life as well as on the stage, passion is a manifestation of personal energy and an exigence of personal development, and the pursuit of glory is motivated by irrational drives which, as contemporary moralists recognized, go beyond the norms of reason. After the setback suffered by the aristocracy at the time of the Fronde, which was followed by their domestication to the absolute authority of Louis XIV, the ethic of glory was supplanted by the ethic of *honnêteté*, an ideal of civilized living aspired to by leisured bourgeois and nobleman alike. In the writings of its chief theorists, the Chevalier de Méré (1609–84) and Damien Miton, it emerges as an ethic of enlightened self-interest, such as Philinte urges on Alceste in Molière's *Misanthrope*, the end of which is the achievement of a harmonious society composed of people of cultivated good manners who find their own happiness in the happiness of others.

Blaise Pascal (1623–62) is outstanding among seventeenth-century authors as the acutest critic of the rationalistic tendencies we have so far described, and (in the opinion of many) the profoundest thinker of the entire century. He was a mathematician of genius and a scientist whose experimental practice was far in advance of his time, as well as an inventor, and a man who, at one time, frequented the company of the spokesmen of *honnêteté*, Méré and Miton. He was therefore well placed to judge both the deeper implications of mechanism and the tendencies of ethical thought in his day. Pascal wrote from a religious standpoint which was both intensely personal and in close sympathy with the views of the Jansenists of Port-Royal, who published the posthumous fragments of Pascal's projected defence of Christianity, known as the *Pensées*, in 1670. It was for a long time thought that Pascal's notes were in too much disarray for it to be possible to reconstruct the plan of his intended *Apologie*, but modern scholarship has shown that we can at least recover the provisional order in which the author had classified his material at the time of his death. Pascal put his finger on the weakness of Descartes's apparently orthodox separation of the domains of faith and reason which, given the philosopher's emphasis on the certainties to be attained by deductive reasoning, could only push revealed religion further and further into the margin of life. Although he failed to do justice to Descartes's reasons for introducing God into his system – he needed God, Pascal claimed, only in order to give the universe an initial push to set it in motion – he accurately foresaw that by reducing the universe to matter and movement, Cartesianism would be held to render revealed religion unnecessary and lead simply to deism. Pascal himself was convinced that the Christian revelation alone could make coherent sense of the human experience, and this is the central theme of the *Pensées*. He was writing for the intelligent agnostic of his day, a man influenced by Montaigne while in touch with the main developments in scientific thought, and he drew heavily on both Montaigne and science for persuasive imagery. He credits man with a desire for truth and happiness which, since it is beyond unregenerate human nature, causes him to relapse into scepticism and the pursuit of distracting activities ('le divertissement') which represent an unconscious attempt to escape from the anxiety inseparable from a true knowledge of the human condition. Only the Christian doctrine of the Fall and Redemption can make sense of the human dilemma, and only the grace mediated by the Roman Catholic religion, which alone has the truth, can offer an escape from it. Pascal's argument is impressive even to those who accept neither the diagnosis nor the cure. In particular, it contrasts advantageously with the moral and demonstrative proofs of natural theology offered by the overwhelming majority of seventeenth-century apologists. Pascal eschews such proofs. Even the notorious argument of the Wager, in which he attempts to persuade the reader, on the basis of an application of the calculus of probabilities, of the advantage of believing that God exists, is not presented as a proof, but as a means of encouraging the reader to commit his entire personality, and not simply his intellect, to the search for belief. In this as in his exploitation of the theme of anxiety, Pascal anticipates modern existentialism. Despite his attitude to proofs, Pascal is not an anti-rationalist, as the Romantics chose to think, largely on the basis of their misinterpretation of the term 'le cœur' and their disregard for the fact that 'la raison' is one of Pascal's 'trois moyens de croire'. He deliberately cites 'proofs' drawn from scriptural evidence of the fulfilment of prophecies, which illustrate the continuity of the Old and New Testaments and provide a figurative expression of the universality of Christian doctrine, because they are not demonstrative: if therefore the reader is convinced by them, it must be because his intellect has been illuminated by divine grace.

Pascal here writes not as a fideist (as it might seem) but as an Augustinian Christian, prepared to admit the possibility of rational demonstrations of natural theology, but denying that they are of any value in bringing a man to faith. Pascal's criticisms of the self-regarding nature of all contemporary ethical doctrines – he includes Stoicism, Epicureanism, the ethic of glory, and *honnêteté* in his condemnation – are made from the same standpoint, as are his views on the social order which he represents as the result of original sin and a necessary punishment imposed by God, thus precluding any serious possibility of reform. Augustinianism is an important factor in seventeenth-century French thought. Its most influential representatives (though far from the only ones) were the small group of clerics and laymen known as the Jansenists because they were followers of the Belgian bishop Jansenius, who died in 1638, two years before the publication of his commentary on St Augustine's theology, the *Augustinus*. While Augustinianism itself can be broadly distinguished from the mainstream of modern Catholic theology, by its strong emphasis on the infirmity of human nature as a result of the Fall, and on the inscrutability of God's plans for the salvation of the individual, Jansenism eludes close definition, since it was an intellectual tendency rather than a specific doctrine, despite the points on which the Pope condemned the *Augustinus* in 1649, but which the Jansenists never admitted they held. Jansenism is often equated with Calvinism, but the leading Jansenist theologians, Antoine Arnauld and Pierre Nicole, were among the most effective of the contemporary controversialists who undertook to write against Calvinism. The stress laid by the Jansenists on a personal experience of conversion (such as Pascal himself underwent) and on rigorous moral standards is not after all the sole prerogative of Protestantism, while the Jansenists consistently gave proof of their orthodoxy in upholding the specifically Catholic doctrine of the Church as the visible communion of the faithful and the essential source of grace through the sacraments.

The Jansenists were at the forefront of a reaction against the aristocratic, optimistic and humanistic tendencies in contemporary ethical thought, which set in during the middle years of the seventeenth century. They particularly denounced the dominance of the self-regarding motive of *amour-propre* and the absence of the theological virtue of charity or *amour de Dieu*. *Amour-propre* was also treated in the *Maximes* (1664) of La Rochefoucauld, who combined acute insight into subconscious motivation with a positive belief in the moral values associated with the ethic of *honnêteté*. However, the Jansenists' own view of the subconscious workings of *amour-propre* led Nicole, in his *Essais de Morale* (1671–80), to the extreme conclusion that we have no objective means of distinguishing between virtuous and sinful acts. Against this, their bitterest enemies the Jesuits (already accused by Pascal, in his *Lettres provinciales* (1656–7) of condoning lax standards of morality) stressed man's natural capacity to know and do God's will, and counted as sinful only acts done in conscious awareness that a moral law was being broken.

Pascal's critique of both Cartesian rationalism and mundane ethics proved ineffectual so far as the next generation was concerned. His 'proofs' of Christianity, relying as they did in contemporary eyes on an orthodox (i.e. literal) as well as a figurative interpretation of the biblical text, were undermined by the modern techniques of biblical criticism initiated by Spinoza who treated the Bible as a work of Jewish history in his *Tractatus theologico-politicus* (1670) and employed by the Oratorian priest Richard Simon in his *Histoire critique du Vieux Testament* (1677). The Port-Royal editors of the *Pensées* had been won over to Cartesianism, and interfered with Pascal's text in order to accommodate the author's thought to their own ideas. Proofs of natural theology borrowed from or modelled on Descartes were used to revive rationalist apologetics. Bossuet (1627–1704), the most impressive and intelligent orthodox defender of Christianity in the seventeenth century, invoked the Cartesian criterion of clearness and distinctness in his *Traité du libre arbitre* (1677) and based the contemporary *Traité de la connaissance de Dieu et de soi-même* (published posthumously) on *Les Passions de l'âme*, but he incorporated Cartesian ideas and demonstrations into the perspective of traditional Augustinian Christianity, while he later saw that Cartesianism offered a threat to religion by subordinating revelation to reason, and he continued to represent the moral rigorism of Pascal and the Jansenists, particularly in his polemics against the theatre, as did Fénelon (1651–1715), another Cartesian so far as his apologetics were concerned, who also inveighed against the increasing tendency of the age to value worldly goods (a major theme of moralist literature, as the expansion of trade and the development of luxury industries altered the nature of the economy) and associated mundane civilization with moral decadence much as Rousseau was to do half a century later. Nevertheless, as Robert Mauzi in particular has shown, the tide was not in their favour. Whereas in the *Pensées* the argument that Christianity is relevant to human experience is used to show the urgent need for grace and salvation, Christian moralists of the eighteenth century begin to present Christianity as 'relevant' in a different sense: Christianity is the best religion, it is claimed, because it is the best suited to procure personal happiness and social harmony. The Christian and the *honnête homme*, far from being opposed ideals as Bossuet preached, thus become almost indistinguishable.

'La Crise de la Conscience'

The last quarter of the seventeenth century and the first half of the eighteenth was first and foremost an age of criticism and reconstruction in which rationalism was used not only to undermine traditional authority, but also as a means of discovering man's basic needs and aspirations and the institutions which would enable him to satisfy them. This is the period of the 'crisis of the European conscience', and subsequently of the emergence of the *philosophe*, a man who was not only a philosopher, but a critic and a social reformer. The 'crisis of conscience' was perhaps not so much a crisis as a growing awareness of the corrosive powers of reason when applied to the dead wood of tradition. The motives of those who used reason critically were by no means clear-cut, and they often continued to respect the framework of Christian belief within which their targets fell. The *philosophes*, on the other hand, deliberately used reason to undermine established authority, fostering the movement of the Enlightenment, in which the purpose of knowledge was to liberate men's minds in order that they should enjoy happiness in the here and now, which meant open opposition to the exclusive Roman Catholic Church and the despotic outlook of the absolute monarchy. This period also germinated the concept of *sensibilité* which flowered, often over-luxuriantly, throughout the eighteenth century. To be a true human being no longer meant that a man successfully exercised reason and will in the pursuit of God's truth and the imitation of His goodness, but that he responded emotionally to the sufferings of others and was thereby moved to acts of charity towards his fellow-men. There was not yet, however, any question of preferring the promptings of the heart to the demands of reason, as was to be the case with the Romantics. Sentiment reinforced reason, restoring something of what reason had lost when its meaning was reduced from 'right reason' which embraced feeling as well as intellect, to its analytical and critical functions. Only later, when reason was further reduced to a mere reflection of sensation, did the cult of *sensibilité* begin to develop into a justification of man's instinctive drives and eventually come to be at odds with normative reason.

When particular cases are considered, it is not easy to draw a firm line between the *philosophes* and their precursors, between freethinking within a Christian context and that which carries its authors (whether consciously or not it is often hard to say) into direct opposition to the Christian basis of the social order. The plans of Vauban (*La Dîme royale*, 1707) for fiscal reform and those of Fénelon, tutor to successive heirs to the throne, for administrative reform and a relaxation of absolutism (*Tables de Chaulnes*, written in 1711), are attempts to reform the regime from within. Similarly, the celebrated *Caractères, ou les mœurs de ce siècle*, by La Bruyère (1645–96), published between 1688 and 1696, are the work of a man who, while acutely critical of particular abuses, remains a supporter of the divine right of monarchy and the Roman Catholic Church to the extent of vituperating against the Protestant usurper of the English throne, William of Orange, and approving Louis XIV's revocation of the Edict of Nantes in 1685 which resulted in the persecution and flight into exile of his Protestant subjects. Saint-Évremond, on the other hand, comes close to the outlook of the *philosophes* when he speaks of William of Orange as the example of an enlightened monarch and of the Revocation as an offence against humanity. Even so, he writes from within a Christian context, envisaging toleration as a stage on the way to Christian reunion. We are reminded of Erasmus more than of Voltaire.

The case of Pierre Bayle (1647–1706) is more complex. In his early *Pensées diverses sur la comète* (1682–3) he methodically exposed (in a manner which owes something to the example of Cartesian logic) the irrationality of the popular, and pious, superstition that comets are divinely inspired phenomena which presage or cause changes in human affairs. He then digressed on to the thesis that a society of atheists, supposing one to exist, would be as virtuous as a society of Christians. The *philosophes* thought that Bayle was claiming that morality is independent of belief, and were shocked or delighted according to their particular tendencies, but modern scholars argue that in order to understand Bayle's point we should replace his thought in the context of contemporary Calvinist polemics in which, as a French Calvinist who had fled into exile in Holland, he was personally involved. The digression can then be read as an attack on Roman Catholics, who are lumped together with pagan idolators as an inferior category to both Calvinists and atheists. Bayle's greatest work is his *Dictionnaire historique et critique* (1697; 2nd edition, 1702). With its anodyne text and provocative, immensely learned footnotes in which every opinion on the subject in hand is cited and shown to conflict, it becomes more intelligible if it is interpreted in a similar way. However, Bayle can hardly be called a Calvinist apologist, as some scholars have claimed. Contemporary Calvinists divided into two camps, orthodox and 'liberal'. The former believed in blind faith and coercion, the latter in a rational search for truth and in religious toleration. Bayle offended both parties by defending blind faith while championing toleration. His dialectic technique seems to have been aimed at driving the orthodox, convinced of their election, back within the retrenchments of their faith, thus preventing them from harming their opponents who, in their turn, were required by Bayle to abandon the use of reason in theology because it was inevitably corrosive of faith. Religious toleration, which Bayle regarded as the highest requirement of Christian morality, is the real beneficiary of this strategy.

With Fontenelle (1657–1757) we are much closer to the *philosophes*.

Fontenelle's *Histoire des oracles* (1686), like Bayle's work on comets, debunks a popular superstition, namely the belief that the pagan oracles were inspired by demons, supernatural beings whose voice was miraculously silenced by the birth of Christ. Fontenelle shows the influence of Cartesian logic when he takes the documentary evidence in the case, reconstitutes it into the chains of reasoning which are supposed to support the belief, and shows that these fall apart when rigorous standards of proof are applied. His conclusion that the oracles were 'worked' by their priests gave fresh life to the *libertin* thesis that religious institutions are man-made. Fontenelle was able to claim that leading ecclesiastics, and not simply *libertins*, were in favour of stripping Christian teaching of such superstitious accretions. His own view of religion appears wholly detached and analytical. A noteworthy example is his *De l'origine des fables* (written in the 1690s, published 1724) where he puts forward the thesis that men have created divinities in their own image as a result of a fundamental disposition of the human mind to explain the unknown by the known. This psychological analysis of the origins of religious belief was taken further by the eighteenth-century materialists, notably Helvétius who was a great admirer of Fontenelle. Fontenelle's *Entretiens sur la pluralité des mondes* (1686) is noteworthy, despite factual errors, as a delightful popularization of the Copernican system and Cartesian physics, but perhaps the feature in it most indicative of the author's mentality is the way he substitutes the sentiment of joy in scientific discovery for the anguish and religious awe with which Pascal believed man should react to 'le silence de ces espaces infinis'.

Montesquieu (1689–1755) is the first author to whom historians normally accord the title of *philosophe*. His *Lettres persanes* (1721) is a brilliant example of the way the confrontation of two cultures was used not only to inculcate a lesson of relativism – and thus dislodge from the French reader's mind the conviction that only French ideas and institutions are valid – but also to point to the universality of deistic belief and the idea of natural justice. Deism may be defined as belief in a God who is the creator of the world, and whose existence is known by reason without the need for revelation. The deists accept the complete adequacy of the moral law laid down in the Gospels, which reduces to the requirement to practise justice and charity. This is the only divine command, and there is no need for priests, dogmas or ceremonies. The seeds of deism were sown in the seventeenth century, in the philosophers' proofs of God as the efficient cause of the universe, in the use of reason to criticize revealed doctrine and, perhaps more than anything else, the revulsion felt by many Christians at the intolerant acts committed in the name of doctrinaire beliefs, which led them to subordinate doctrine to ethics, and to preach toleration. Deism was also fostered by the discovery of foreign cultures, notably in the East, which showed that men could be devout believers in God and lead moral lives without the benefit of the Christian revelation and its dogmas. The same sources helped to foster a similar, if more discreet, lesson of social criticism, showing that stable government and the happiness and prosperity of the individual could be achieved without despotic rule, and with a minimum of imposed authority. When the foreign culture was not authentically discovered, it was invented, hence the popular stories concerning the voyages of Frenchmen to fictitious Utopias, such as Gabriel de Foigny's *La Terre australe connue* (1676) and Denis Veiras's *Histoire des Sévarambes* (1677). Like his precursor Marana, the author of *L'Espion dans les cours* (1684), Montesquieu scored by bringing his foreign travellers to France, and by thorough documentation of the visitors' background.

Montesquieu's greatest contribution to French thought was in the field of political ideas. In *Lettres persanes* his characters discuss seriously the problem of the best form of government, and look in particular to England where monarchs who rule arbitrarily are deposed or executed, but the monarchy remains a respected institution. Bossuet had seen in this a sign of the inherent political instability of the English nation, but for Montesquieu the English have an enviable secret. The clue (or so he thought) was later given him by Bolingbroke, who assured him that the basis of the English monarchy was the separation of powers and division of sovereignty among the legislative, executive and judiciary bodies. Montesquieu incorporated this erroneous notion into his major work, *De l'esprit des lois* (1748), whence it passed into the American Constitution. Both in *Lettres persanes* and in *De l'esprit des lois*, however, Montesquieu harks back to the myth of the 'good old days' when the French king supposedly shared his power and responsibilities with the nobility in an ideal feudal society. The feudal myth had already inspired other discontented aristocrats, including Fénelon and the memorialist Saint-Simon, who published his *Histoire de l'ancien gouvernement de France* in 1727. In the main, however, *De l'esprit des lois* strikes a remarkable balance between the idea of a rational, universal principle of justice providing a yardstick with which to judge the positive laws by which a nation is governed, and recognition of the multifarious causes which make positive legislation evolve. Montesquieu showed himself in this to be one of the first thinkers of his day to recognize that the world in which he lived was not a static but a developing one.

Voltaire (1694–1778) dominates the entire *philosophe* movement, but it is not wholly arbitrary to see his career as dividing into two periods, one before and one after 1750. His fervent commitment to the righting of particular wrongs, and his battle against the Infamous Beast of clerical and political tyranny, date from after 1750. Before that date he was the pungent satirist of *Lettres philosophiques* (1734) and the somewhat complacent moralist of *Le Mondain* (1736) as well as, as will be seen, the French champion of Locke and Newton. *Lettres philosophiques*, in its critical aspects, inculcates the lesson of deism as *Lettres persanes* had done. It also offers the French reader object lessons, drawn from the example of his nearest neighbour, of how intellectual, religious and political affairs should be conducted. The boldest section of the work is probably that in which the author shows that the price of liberty, if reform is not put in hand from within, may be civil war and even regicide. This is the most inflammatory passage in any published work of the period, although similar sentiments had been expressed in the *Mémoire* or *Testament* of the atheist parish priest Jean Meslier (1678–1733), copies of which were in circulation in the late 1720s. Voltaire later edited and published Meslier's work in a somewhat watered-down form.

All the authors we have been considering were critical of metaphysical speculation, which they regarded as useless, and none more so than Voltaire who never tired of condemning the bogus profundity and obscure jargon, as he saw it, of the professional philosophers. Nevertheless, the period was rich in speculative philosophy, which influenced even those who appeared most scornful of it. Cartesian rationalism received an original development in the work of Malebranche and Leibniz: the latter, although not a Frenchman, wrote some of his works in French and soon became influential in France. English thought, represented by Locke and later by Newton, constituted another important foreign influence. Finally, there was a remarkable revival of naturalism, which seemed at first to have been eclipsed by the success of mechanism.

Nicolas Malebranche (1638–1715) was an Oratorian priest whose main work is the *Recherche de la vérité* (1675–6). Instead of simply drawing on Cartesianism for apologetic purposes as Bossuet and

Fénelon had done, he set out to make it into a religious philosophy. The greatest difficulty he, along with other late seventeenth-century rationalists, found in Cartesianism was the distinction of the two 'substances', thought and matter, and more particularly the problem of their interaction. Malebranche replaced Descartes's solution by the doctrine of 'occasionalism' which had been put forward by a Belgian Cartesian, Arnold Guelincx (1625–69). Occasionalism states that our decision to act is not the real cause of the action: the decision and the action are simultaneously caused by a decision by God to put His laws of motion into operation. Although occasionalism required God to perform a continual series of miracles, this was a better alternative, in Malebranche's view, than going back to the naturalist concept of an inherent 'vital force' which is responsible for the movement of physical objects. Malebranche also criticized Descartes's theory of innate ideas. It was implausible of Descartes to suggest that the mind could contain every conceivable idea it might ever have, and illogical of him to claim that the presence of an object could be the cause of an idea, even in the limited sense of triggering off one that was already in the mind. Only God can be the real source of our ideas, giving us a mental picture of the object on each 'occasion' on which our senses are confronted with it. In Malebranche's phrase, we 'see everything in God', who alone has true knowledge of things. God, for Malebranche, was above all the source of order in the universe. The concept of order as the ground of all truth and wisdom dominates his thought. The religious application of his philosophy is based on a clear distinction between the realms of nature and grace, a subject treated in his *Traité de la nature et de la grâce* (1680). The fact that we do not always have clear and distinct ideas, or make decisions and have desires which are in harmony with the ideal of order God has set before us in the physical universe, is due to the corruption of reason and will as a result of the Fall, and points to the need for salvation which, however, is not the work of natural reason but of recourse to God's revealed word in Scripture and the traditions of the Church.

Malebranche's is the most successful attempt to harmonize revealed Christianity and mechanistic science, and was more effective than Descartes's own philosophy in presenting the universe of the mechanists as an object of devout contemplation. Malebranche's influence has never been fully documented, but it was clearly immense. His theory of the origins of error is echoed in Fontenelle's *De l'origine des fables*; his theism impressed Bayle and saved him from complete scepticism;

Voltaire ridiculed his doctrine of 'seeing things in God', but found that he was hard put to it to improve on it when he came to write the article 'Idée' in his own *Dictionnaire philosophique*. It was Malebranche, as much as the natural law jurists of the seventeenth century, who influenced Montesquieu's belief that the unvarying operations of nature revealed by science should constitute a model for human affairs. Like Malebranche, Montesquieu acknowledges that it is human infirmity which stands in the way of this ideal; where he differs is in turning to science rather than to religion for a remedy, for in *De l'esprit des lois* Montesquieu adopts towards society the same standpoint as the physical scientist with his knowledge of the workings of cause and effect.

Leibniz (1646–1716) took much the same starting-point for his philosophy as Malebranche had done, but against Malebranche he held that the synchronism of mind and body is pre-established. God has fixed once and for all the laws which govern movement in the physical universe, and relate thought and action, and so does not need to perform a continual series of miracles. But his greatest influence on French thought in the first part of the eighteenth century came through his *Essais de Théodicée*, written in French and published in 1710. Leibniz's work was a reply to Bayle's pessimistic contention that evil is inherent in nature, and only intelligible if we accept the heretical Manichean view that the fate of mankind is the subject of a perpetual tug of war between the equal and opposing forces of God and the Devil. Leibniz argued that in order not to simply reduplicate Himself, God had necessarily to create a finite world which fell short of perfection in every one of its parts; nevertheless, each part belongs to a harmonious plan, and we only see evil because we cannot grasp the contribution of the part to the general good. Leibniz's solution to the problem of reconciling the existence of a just God with the fact of evil and suffering in the world was popularized by Pope in his *Essay on Man*. In this form it influenced Voltaire whose earlier works, notably the last of the *Lettres philosophiques* where he attacks Pascal's view of the human condition, and the poem *Le Mondain* where he gives voice to a somewhat complacent view of the pleasures of existence, express a point of view against which he later reacted. Other aspects of Leibniz's thought, especially those concerned with the sensitivity of matter, and his profound understanding of movement as a process of organic change rather than mechanical displacement, were not taken up by French thinkers until the second half of the eighteenth century.

Voltaire regarded Malebranche, and later came to regard Leibniz, as the epitome of the professional philosopher who dresses up useless abstractions in pretentious jargon. His own sympathies went to the more down-to-earth English philosophers who restricted themselves to what could be verified by observation, Locke and Newton. Locke's work, the *Essay on Human Understanding* (1690), was in fact well known in France long before Voltaire praised it. It had been publicized in a long article in the *Bibliothèque universelle* two years before it appeared in print, and had inspired a systematic work of philosophy, the Jesuit Father Buffier's *Traité des premières vérités* (1724), which Voltaire himself admired. Locke's theory of knowledge, which made thought dependent on material supplied by the senses, the senses being the source and not simply the occasion of our ideas, was widely held to have refuted Descartes's doctrine of innate ideas. Locke's sensationalism also reinforced the empirical scientific method of Newton, whose *Principia* (1687) completely contradicted the premises and conclusions of Cartesian physics, notably in the case of the movement of the heavenly bodies, which Newton ascribed to gravitational attraction across empty space. Here the English influence was markedly less successful. Cartesian physics had, it is true, moved some way towards empiricism. Whereas Descartes made reason alone the means of scientific discovery, his disciples referred to experience. But experience meant to them common-sense observations rather than controlled experiment. In his *Traité de physique* (1671), the most representative work of post-Cartesian physics, Jacques Rohault defended the theory that all movement in the universe is that of particles of matter moving under impulsion in a series of whirlpools; but he did so not, as Descartes himself had done, by arguing that since extended substance is solid matter, any other form of movement is metaphysically inconceivable, but on the grounds that common sense tells us that objects only do move when they are impelled. The same point of view was adopted by Fontenelle who, in the influential post of permanent secretary of the Académie des Sciences, effectively prevented the discussion of Newton's theories in scientific circles. Newton's idea of gravitational attraction seemed to Fontenelle to be a mere name for something that could not be explained mechanically, a throwback to the 'occult causes' of the scholastics. This view prevailed until Voltaire, prompted by Maupertuis, one of the few Newtonians in the Académie, successfully argued that a concept which could be expressed in a mathematical formula of such complete generality, and from which the correct results always followed, must represent a 'real' phenomenon in nature.

Voltaire was aware that the ideas of both Locke and Newton could be given a materialist interpretation. He flirted with materialism when discussing these thinkers in *Lettres philosophiques* and in his unpublished *Traité de métaphysique* (written 1734), before coming out against it in *Éléments de la philosophie de Newton* (1737). Materialism did not attain the status of a coherent philosophy until after 1750 when, as we shall see, French thinkers achieved a remarkable adumbration of the modern idea of evolution. The concept was, however, as old as antiquity, and the Epicurean philosophy which Gassendi revived and made respectable in the seventeenth century was originally a materialist system. In the last years of the century, materialism was given a new impetus by the development of Cartesianism. Descartes had set side by side a finite universe of matter in motion, and an immaterial realm of thought. The temptation existed to swallow one up in the other, and to make matter a subjective perception of the soul, or thought an aspect of matter. The former way was taken in England by Bishop Berkeley (1685–1753), but he had little influence in France. French thinkers did, however, draw a materialist philosophy out of Cartesianism, representing the universe as a self-sustaining system of matter in motion which did not require the idea of God to support it. This version of Cartesianism was confused with the philosophy of Spinoza. In his *Ethics*, posthumously published in 1677, Spinoza held that there are not two substances, as Descartes had claimed, but one; that God cannot be a cause outside nature, but must be immanent in nature; that nature, in all its aspects, is the manifestation of God. Spinoza's philosophy, though extremely influential, was almost wholly misunderstood until the very end of the eighteenth century. Some thought that like the 'nouveaux cartésiens' he had eliminated God from nature; others that in affirming God's immanence in nature, he had revived the naturalist doctrine of the world soul. Naturalist ideas had been kept alive in France by Gassendi (despite his mechanistic astronomy), by Cyrano de Bergerac, and in the *Essais de physique* (1677) of Gassendi's disciple Gilles de Launay. After 1680, they were reinforced by accounts of oriental religions in which a concept similar to that of the world soul was said to be found; in the eighteenth century naturalism was further propagated through the influence of the English writer John Toland, whose *Letters to Serena* (1704) and *Pantheisticon* (1720) were known in France, and through the works of the Italian Francesco Colonna (1644–1726) who spent most of his life in France. According to Colonna there are two kinds of matter, one insensible, and the other capable of motion and feeling. He distinguished between plants, animals and men solely in terms of their capacity for feeling. Both naturalist and Cartesian varieties of 'Spinozism' were propagated above all in the numerous treatises which, throughout the early part of the eighteenth century, circulated clandestinely in manuscript copies: more than a hundred of these are extant, in over four hundred copies.

The ideas of Locke and Newton were indirectly drawn into this movement towards materialism. In a digressive passage of his *Essay on Human Understanding* Locke had raised the question whether matter can think and had concluded that God could, if he wished, 'super-add' thought to matter. Voltaire used this in *Lettres philosophiques* merely to embarrass the theologians, but in the clandestine *Mémoire* of Jean Meslier it was given a 'Spinozist' bias. In similar vein, Newton spoke of gravity as a property not inherent in matter, which God had nevertheless given to matter. This raised the question: why should it not be inherent in matter? What the orthodox Cartesian scientists denounced as a regression to the 'occult causes' of scholastic philosophy began to be regarded by others as 'occult' in a different sense – one of nature's secrets, not God's. The only way to solve the mystery was to 'approfondir l'idée que nous avons de la matière'. These words of d'Alembert constitute the whole basis of the new journey of intellectual discovery on which the *philosophes* embarked in the 1740s and 1750s.

The *Philosophe* Movement

By 1750 the *philosophe* movement could be said to have come of age. This was certainly the belief of the editors and contributors who were responsible for the great *Encyclopédie ou dictionnaire raisonné des sciences et des arts* (vols 1–7, 1751–7; vols 8–17, 1765), which has been called the epitome of the Enlightenment. The avowed aim of the editors, Diderot and d'Alembert, was to 'changer la manière *commune* de penser', and this meant to a large extent consolidating existing gains rather than opening up new horizons. Montesquieu's views find a large place in the political articles mostly contributed by his disciple Jaucourt, while the work as a whole assumes that Voltaire's deism, with its emphasis on toleration and reason and its satire of revelation, priestly cults and unnecessary dogmas, is the norm among 'reasonable men'. Occasionally, however, its pages reflect the bolder views which found full expression in the remarkable crop of publications, beginning in the 1740s, in which authors such as Maupertuis, La Mettrie, Robinet,

Buffon, D'Holbach, Helvétius and, above all, Diderot, adumbrated a materialist philosophy which eventually split the *philosophe* movement, alienating two of its most outstanding figures, Voltaire himself and Rousseau. Setting aside the hesitations in their views and the divergences of detail between the different authors, the materialists can be seen to share a common conviction: that while Locke and Newton have laid the foundations of a true theory of knowledge and an accurate scientific method, they have not (as Voltaire believed) said the last word on all that men need to know; that the search for truth can only proceed by setting aside the metaphysical concepts of God and the spiritual soul; that reason and observation make us conclude that the universe is not a static mechanism created by a purposive deity, but a self-sustaining system of matter in perpetual transformation, in which man himself is, like all other forms of life, an evolutionary product of his material environment.

The *philosophes* reached this conclusion through brilliant conjecture based on the growing body of knowledge concerning the life sciences, notably geology, botany and biology. Geological research pointed to the great changes which had taken place in the earth's crust, and indicated that the fossils found in rock strata were evidence that the forms of life had evolved over an immense period of time; Linnaeus's classification of plants by their distinguishing features also showed the difficulty of drawing firm boundaries between the species, while geneticists proposed that all species could in fact be derived by differentiation from a common pair of ancestors; practical observations and experiments showed that the animal and vegetable realms were continuous, and also that some species were self-regenerating. The mechanical model which had served so well in astronomy and physics now appeared inadequate to deal with this evidence of the inner dynamism of organic life, and to answer the fundamental questions which the life sciences raised concerning the origins of life, the variety of species, the principle of their reproduction and growth, and even the question of the connection between inert and living matter. The French materialists made an important break with the mechanism of their predecessors. Although explanations of a mechanical type loom large in Maupertuis's ideas on natural selection, in La Mettrie's physiology, and in D'Holbach's biology, these writers knew that before they could give a satisfactory account of the phenomena which they were trying to interpret, it was first necessary to discover the primary qualities of matter, so as to know what it was that had to be measured. Thus they allowed themselves to be stimulated by the naturalist tradition, opposed to mechanism: this had kept alive the notions of the universal sensitivity of matter and the diffusion throughout nature of an animating principle, which Diderot was eventually to reinterpret in a more truly scientific manner.

The French materialists provoked much the same kind of opposition from the Church as Darwin's documentation of the evolutionary theory in the *Origin of Species* was to do in England a century later. There is of course no reason of principle why a materialistic, evolutionary science should not coexist, as it often does today, with religious faith. The *philosophes* themselves did not become materialists in order to advance the cause of atheism, as is sometimes said; they attacked religion because the religious account of the universe was in conflict with the facts as they observed them, and incompatible with the further progress of scientific knowledge. They were not in fact all atheists. If the position of Buffon in his great *Histoire naturelle* (1749–88) or of Robinet in *De la nature* (1761) is equivocal, Charles Bonnet's *La palingénésie philosophique* (1770) reads like something by Teilhard de Chardin in its rhapsodic description of man's advance up the evolutionary ladder to ultimate union with God. Nor were leading ecclesiastics always happy about the repression of truth to which the Church committed itself when it had Diderot imprisoned, subjected Montesquieu's *De l'esprit des lois* to censure on the grounds of 'Spinozism', condemned Helvétius's *De l'esprit*, and held up the publication of the *Encyclopédie* for seven years, or with the obscurantist insistence by religious apologists that the whole history of creation, and of the origins of life, the truths of geology, biology and even astronomy (Copernicus's works were still on the Roman Catholic Index of prohibited books) were all literally recorded in the Bible. Yet all this is understandable when we recall that the materialist *philosophes*, in contradicting the literal account of the creation in the first chapter of *Genesis*, were removing at one blow the whole basis of the Church's authority over men's lives, and the very foundations of the faith that still sustained the majority of Frenchmen even if it had become largely meaningless to the educated élite.

In their doctrine of man, the materialist *philosophes* stressed the dependence of the mind on physical causes and held that all actions are physically determined. They were disciples of Locke, but whereas Locke had maintained that some operations of the mind are innate, his French followers believed that ideas are only a reflection of objects perceived by the senses. In his *Traité des sensations* (1754), Condillac denied that the mind contains any principle of rationality which interprets the evidence of the senses, and he defined the mind as an agglomeration of ideas which were once sense impressions. Helvétius went further, in defining man, in *De l'esprit* (1758), as a pleasure-seeking and pain-avoiding animal whose ideas are the result of his environment. The materialists further rejected in the name of the laws of mechanical causality the Christian idea of free will, which presupposes a spiritual soul free, under grace (and to an extent dependent on one's particular theological views), to accept or refuse God's commands independently of material contingency. Once the theological notion of free will was discarded, the concepts of 'virtue' and 'vice' as normally understood could be said to be meaningless: men, according to Diderot, are not virtuous or vicious, but fortunately or unfortunately born. The materialists' determinism did not, however, make them into fatalists. True devotees of Enlightenment, they held that knowledge of the causes which determined human thought and action should be employed to the end of personal happiness and the social good. This brings us to one of the most interesting aspects of the thought of this period – the tension between the determinism of the *philosophes* and their moral idealism.

Although sometimes obscured by the ambiguity of the term 'nature', which could refer either to a system of material causes or to a moral norm, this tension came increasingly to the fore as time went on. The real dilemma facing the *philosophes* was that of reconciling the social end they believed to be appropriate to man, with their equally convinced belief in the natural right of the individual to give free play to his instinctive energies. On the one hand, they stressed the role of social engineering, the possibility of using education, public opinion, the laws and punishments to 'modify' the man who was unfortunately born in order to coerce him into becoming a useful member of society. On the other hand, they rehabilitated the passions, protesting against Christian asceticism and the miseries to which its inhibitions gave rise, and representing the passions not simply as the motive force of acts of benevolence, but as the sign of a healthy material organism. La Mettrie in his *Traité du bonheur* (1748) and much later in the century the Marquis de Sade (1740–1814) in his novels *Justine* (1795) and *La Nouvelle Juliette* (1797), pointed up the difficulty: since man is a part of nature ('un être formé par la nature et circonscrit par elle', as D'Holbach wrote), then everything he does must be natural; why then, if a man is so constituted as to find pleasure in crime, should he be punished? Sade's provocative depiction of the trials of virtue and the triumphs of vice may not be sufficient to make him the representative figure some scholars claim, but his work provides a valuable counter to the optimism of those authors who, ignoring the realities of life around them, declared that man was steadily and inevitably progressing towards perfect happiness and social harmony, a view nobly expressed under the shadow of the guillotine by Condorcet in his *Esquisse d'un tableau historique des progrès de l'esprit humain* (posth. 1795).

The most doctrinaire statement of materialism is D'Holbach's *Système de la nature* (1770). D'Holbach (1723–89), an Alsatian nobleman, is important for his translations of foreign scientific publications, for his numerous scientific contributions to the *Encyclopédie*, for the violent diatribes which he wrote in support of Voltaire's campaign against the Infamous Beast of clerical oppression and despotism, for his part in the publication of the clandestine manuscripts which had circulated earlier in the century, and in particular for grouping round him most of the major thinkers of his day in what became known as the 'côterie holbachienne'. The most outstanding figure, however, was Denis Diderot (1713–84), who was more tentative but also more open-minded than D'Holbach, and who ranks with Voltaire and Rousseau as one of the three great figures in eighteenth-century thought. It was he who gave the most boldly imaginative and the most prophetic account of the evolutionary theory. Diderot succeeded both in locating the principle of organic change in the structure of matter itself, and in defining the true experimental method. Thus he was able, while being inspired by the vitalist concept in naturalism, to purge naturalism of its pre-scientific and magical associations. He never ceased to develop intellectually, as can be seen if we trace his ideas through from the *Pensées philosophiques* (1746) and *Lettre sur les aveugles* (1749) via the *Pensées sur l'interprétation de la nature* (1754) and his contributions to the *Encyclopédie*, to the fascinating set of dialogues known as the *Rêve de d'Alembert* (written 1769, publ. posth.). In these works, Diderot anticipated not only the Mendelian theory of genetic inheritance and the Darwinian doctrine of natural selection (in both of which he had Maupertuis as a precursor), but also much of the modern theory of matter, including the notions of potential and kinetic energy, the atom and the cell. In the *Pensées sur l'interprétation de la nature* he gave a classic definition of the experimental method, stressing the need for imaginative hypotheses as well as well-devised experiments tested by accurate observations, in a way that avoids the pitfalls of a narrow 'Baconian' kind of empiricism, and the temptations of the Cartesian 'esprit de système'. Even so, his keenest concern was with moral problems, and he pondered more deeply than any of his contemporaries the eighteenth-century dilemma of the individual and the social. He agreed with his fellow materialists on the need for social engineering, but was distressed by the tendency of some of them to depersonalize human beings. He particularly objected to Helvétius's claim that since the differences between individuals are entirely due to environment, they can be levelled out by education: Diderot stressed instead the inherited nature of mental and moral characteristics. He showed an unusual awareness of the role of unconscious mentality, and was particularly sensitive to the moral problems posed by the presence of physically or psychologically abnormal individuals in society, and especially by the genius who might have to be considered to be above the law if he were not to be deprived of his special qualities. Diderot further objected to Helvétius that the doctrine that everything in nature is a sensitive organism does not imply that the needs of a man are the same as those of an oyster or a plant: 'Je suis homme, et il me faut des causes propres à l'homme'. Man is a complex organism, whose consciousness is not simply a bundle of sensations. He differs from the machine or the animal in possessing reason, and reason is more than a highly evolved form of instinct. In the *Rêve* Diderot drew on recent discoveries of brain surgery to affirm that man is a psycho-physiological unity. He did not try to reduce consciousness to physical changes in the brain, and came close to the modern view that the mind, while it depends on the mechanisms of the brain, harnesses them and is not determined by them.

It is the image of the social reformer, the campaigner against social prejudice, miscarriages of justice, religious intolerance and political tyranny, which is responsible for Voltaire's reputation as the dominant figure among the *philosophes*. The wit and verve of his *contes*, the eloquence of his *Traité sur la tolérance* (1763), the vituperative satire of the *Sermon des cinquante* (1762) and other works aimed at the Infamous Beast, in short the passion with which, from 1749 onwards, Voltaire pursued the practical ends of the Enlightenment, almost persuade one that he deserves it. But his thought is by no means the equal of Diderot's or Rousseau's. Instead of looking upon scepticism, like Diderot, as 'le premier pas vers la vérité', Voltaire was too fond of invoking it as a means of closing the door on further argument. The very title of

Le Philosophe ignorant (1766) betrays this characteristic tendency. Although he enlisted the materialist *philosophes* in his campaign against *l'Infâme*, he was bitterly opposed to their ideas, which he contested point by point, denying that the senses and experience can ever tell us what matter is; that the human mind can penetrate to the causes of phenomena; and that the way in which we interpret nature can affect our knowledge of our moral duties, which comes from God.

Voltaire's positive ideas at this period are best gathered from the *Poème sur la loi naturelle* (1752), the *Dictionnaire philosophique* (1764–5) and the *Histoire de Jenni* (1775), one of his last *contes*, which he wrote with the specific intention of refuting atheism. In these works, Voltaire maintains that everything in nature displays art and purpose, and is the work of a 'divin fabricateur', gives voice to fluctuating opinions on the soul and on free will, first shelves the problem of theodicy in favour of positive action to reduce the amount of suffering in the world, at the time of *Candide* (1759), then finds himself forced to reconsider it when faced with the arguments of D'Holbach's *Système de la nature*. To D'Holbach's contention that Christianity, including its moral teaching, has been the cause of human suffering and crimes, and that man must build his moral code on the basis of observation and experience, Voltaire opposed his deep-rooted conviction that the highest ideas and most authentic motives of morality cannot subsist without belief in God, and that the Christian ethic is the supreme expression of the moral law. In reply to the atheists' argument that the existence of evil and suffering is incompatible with belief in God, Voltaire came close to using the kind of arguments he had derided when satirizing Leibnizian optimism in *Candide*. But the weight of his argument falls on the necessity of belief, not simply in God, but in a God who punishes and rewards in an after-life, if human existence is not to relapse into a state of moral and social anarchy. While his premiss is open to question (though it seemed much less so at a time when all but the most advanced thinkers rejected Bayle's 'paradox' concerning a society of virtuous atheists, than it does today), the genuineness of Voltaire's conviction is undeniable. His is an authentic pragmatism, the only philosophical position, perhaps, logically compatible with the scepticism which remained with him throughout his long career.

Despite his bitter anti-clericalism (which, for a short period in the 1760s, became a violent attack on Christianity and even on the person of Christ), Voltaire thus maintained belief in God and a universal morality against the atheist materialists. The same was true of the third great figure in the *philosophe* movement, Jean-Jacques Rousseau (1712–78). He shared many of the views that the *philosophes* had in common, and he contributed to the *Encyclopédie*, but his relationship with the *philosophes* was uneasy and he finally became convinced that they, as well as the common enemy, the Church, were persecuting him. Attacking Voltaire's deism as an intellectual abstraction and not a lived experience, Rousseau stressed (notably in the *Profession de foi du vicaire savoyard*, 1762) the primacy of inner conviction, and the personal relationship of the individual mind to God over rational argument, although he concurred with the deists' reasons. Like Voltaire, he believed in man's need to act by the inner light of conscience, but he thought of conscience as a God-given principle in the individual rather than as a sense of what is universal in human experience. In all this, he was just as much opposed to the materialists who subjected man to the determinism of physical forces, and the *Profession de foi* is in part a refutation of Helvétius. Rousseau's enthusiastic language and his rehabilitation of religious sentiment do not, as was once believed, make him an anti-rationalist. Reason, conscience and free will are seen by him as a triad of faculties with which God has endowed man so that he can attain perfection. Man's failure to achieve perfection Rousseau blamed on man himself and not, as the *philosophes* tended to do, on the machinations of a self-interested élite of priests and despots.

The central theme of many of his works is the problem of how man, having been thus endowed, has fallen into his present state of subjection to tyranny – in the *Discours sur les sciences et les arts* (1750), to the tyranny of false values nurtured by the kind of technologically orientated civilization which alienates man from his true nature; in the *Discours sur l'origine de l'inégalité* (1755) the tyranny of institutions founded on, and which perpetuate, social inequalities. Although Rousseau's is ultimately a political solution, he approaches it from the standpoint of a moralist. His account of man's degeneration from a hypothetical state of nature in which he was happy and independent, into his present unhappy condition, parallels the biblical account of the Fall and Redemption, but without the doctrine of original sin or the need for a Redeemer other than man himself. Rousseau imagines man as an animal capable of satisfying his instinctive needs so long as external nature does not prevent him, but gifted with the potential for reason which, while it differentiates him from the other animals, cannot be developed until he forms societies. Life in society, however, also develops his passions, and faces him with the problem of translating his original innocence into morality and his independence into the kind of freedom which is compatible with the freedom of others.

In *Du contrat social* (1762), Rousseau goes on to imagine the kind of State men would have set up had they, so to speak, taken the right turning instead of creating, as the second *Discours* describes, the institutions which have enslaved them. The fundamental principle is that of a pact which both seals association and places government in the hands of the entire community – earlier contract theorists had distinguished between a pact of association and one in which the community as a whole gives authority over into the hands of a few of its members. Sovereignty in Rousseau's conception is exercised through a Government which is only an executive agency. The community legislates in the interest of the General Will, a difficult concept which appears to represent a norm of 'rightfulness' inferred from the goodwill which the members of the community ought always to bear to one another. The institutions of Rousseau's ideal State are framed so as to give 'men as they are' the laws they need in order to develop their potential as rational, moral and social beings in accordance with their true nature. Rousseau thus transcends the *philosophes'* dilemma concerning the conflicting claims of social engineering and the free play of personal desires, by calling on men to submit voluntarily to the common rule of the kind of community which will enable them to realize their full potential of virtue. The institutions of his ideal State have been seen by many historians as totalitarian, but Rousseau's conception was not a totalitarian one. If his State is vested with a strong authority over its members it is because, like all the *philosophes*, Rousseau believed that a strong framework of law was necessary to protect individual liberty against the capricious rule of despots: only in comparatively recent times has it been at all widely held that liberty is incompatible with authority, and even that it can only flourish in a state of anarchy.

Du contrat social (little read, incidentally, before the Revolution) was described by one contemporary reader as both useless and dangerous. Useless as a blueprint for practical politics (it requires a community small enough for all the citizens to be able to meet at any time in order to pass legislation – Rousseau's model here was the Swiss cantons rather than his native Geneva), its major premiss that popular sovereignty is the only legitimate basis of government was highly provocative. Other examples of the political thought of the *philosophes* tend to be either more practical or more utopian than Rousseau's conception of the State. In *Lettres philosophiques* Voltaire drew attention to the broad social basis of parliamentary representation in England (which he exaggerated) and to the more equitable system of taxation compared with the French, while Diderot called for a widely based suffrage, to include shopkeepers and farmworkers, together with a form of government which, while exercising strong authority, would protect 'the sacred right of opposition'. But Voltaire also, as a result of his experience of the court of Frederick II of Prussia, supported the idea of enlightened absolutism with the monarch surrounded by *philosophe* advisers, while Montesquieu, as has been seen, wanted to restore the power of former institutions: the ideas of *De l'esprit des lois* tend to support the alliance between the nobility and the magistrates who composed the *parlements* and considered themselves 'the eyes and conscience of the king', which came into being in the course of the eighteenth century. There was not a great deal here which represented a call for radical change and much that positively opposed it. The 'revolutionaries' among the *philosophes* were those like Jean Meslier in his *Mémoire* and Morelly in his *Code de la nature* (1755). The thesis of these works is that men have the choice between slavery and the abolition of private property. This was not a notion likely to carry much practical weight. The major *philosophes*, including even Rousseau, defended the institution of private property, and it has indeed been argued that only the man of property, for which he was unbeholden to a capricious monarch or a feudal overlord, had any chance of initiating the reforms which, rather than a revolutionary upheaval, it was the aim of the movement to bring about.

The *philosophes* were in any case restrained from advocating direct action by their belief (realistic or pessimistic according to one's point of view) that a great many people were, and were bound to remain, ignorant and the slaves of their passions. Some, notably Voltaire, also feared the social consequences of the diminution of the pool of unskilled labour through education. Enlightenment, however far it might or might not be desirable to take it, required in the long run something more than a campaign of pamphlets: it needed a total overhaul of the system of public education, and no Government was likely to initiate sweeping educational reforms which would undermine its own basis. Even after the expulsion of the Jesuit Order from France in 1762, public education remained a mainly clerical monopoly.

The responsibility of the *philosophes* for the Revolution, then, was probably restricted to creating the climate of opinion which made revolution possible. But for many Frenchmen at the time (and for many historians since) the Revolution exemplified the evils of En-lightenment. Paradoxically, their views were not very different from those of Robespierre, who denounced the materialist *philosophes* in the language of Rousseau's Savoyard curate. Both Rousseauism and materialism exerted an influence beyond the Revolution and into the nineteenth century. Rousseau's political writings were, indeed, pillaged to serve the purposes of revolutionary orators and counter-revolution-ary polemicists alike. His greatest influence, however, came through his personal writings, the *Lettres à Malesherbes* (1762), *Rêveries du promeneur solitaire* (1776–8) and *Confessions* (posth. 1781–8). In con-trast to Diderot's scientific approach to the problem of personality, Rousseau studied the nature of the self in his own acts of experience, as had Montaigne; but seeing life exclusively as it was mirrored in his own self-consciousness, he paved the way for Romantic subjectivism, even more than through his sensitivity to the beauties of nature and his morbid enjoyment of emotional and spiritual dissatisfaction, which anticipates the *mal du siècle*.

Romanticism also drew on the materialist tradition to which Rous-seau was opposed. The last years of the eighteenth century witnessed a revival of personal magic and occult philosophy which looks like a throwback to the Renaissance but which was in fact indirectly fostered by the interest the materialists showed in naturalism. Diderot and Swedenborg, different as they were in almost every other respect, both saw nature as a unity, the spiritual being for Swedenborg an extra-ordinary manifestation of the material, perceptible only to an excep-tionally endowed individual. Swedenborg's influence on the Romantics is well known. Authentic scientific materialism continued to flourish: here, Diderot's heirs are Jean-Baptiste Monet (known as Lamarck) whose works straddle the period before and after the Revolution, and who bears the greatest name in the history of evolutionary theory before Darwin, and Pierre-Jean-Georges Cabanis (1757–1808) whose *Rapports du physique et du moral de l'homme* (1802) is one of the classic documents of materialist thought. Cabanis carried on Diderot's interest in the problem of personality, ascribing consciousness to a central ego, identified with the brain which he called 'an organ whose peculiar function is to produce thought'. Cabanis is one of the founders of modern medical psychology; he was also one of the group known as the *idéologues*, who held that social organization can be studied scientifi-cally in terms of the natural laws governing human relationships. In the nineteenth century the *idéologues* influenced the socialist thinker

Henri de Saint-Simon and the philosopher Maine de Biran. These material links, so to speak, between the two centuries, are important. Nevertheless, perhaps the greatest legacy which the whole period with which we have been concerned left to the modern age is to be found in the principles of reason, humanity and toleration, which were never wholly deserted even in the darkest days of the reaction to which the Revolution inevitably gave rise.

Bibliography

In reading further about the topics treated in the foregoing pages, it will be helpful to have at hand a good general history of philosophy, e.g. F. Copleston, *A History of Philosophy*, Vol. 4: *Modern Philosophy from Descartes to Leibniz* (New York, 1963), which is both lucid and comprehensive. The importance of scientific thought in the period is clear, and makes H. Butterfield, *The Origins of Modern Science*, new ed. (London, 1957), essential reading.

There is regrettably no general work on seventeenth-century French thought comparable in quality to those which will be mentioned on the eighteenth century. The symposium on 'La Philosophie au XVIIe siècle' in the periodical *Dix-septième siècle*, nos. 54–5 (Paris, 1962), can, however, be recommended as a helpful introduction. The position for the eighteenth century is very different. The relevant chapters of R. Niklaus, *A Literary History of France: The 18th Century* (London, 1970), constitute an excellent initial guide. Then French thought is brilliantly situated in the context of the general movement of European thought by N. Hampson, *The Enlightenment*, Pelican History of European Thought (Harmondsworth, 1968). These books would form a good approach to J. Ehrard, *L'Idée de nature en France dans la première moitié du 18e siècle* (Paris, 1963 ; republished in an abridged form, 1970), a masterly and original treatment of a whole range of problems extending well beyond both the strict subject of the book and its implied chronological limits. In comparison, E. Cassirer's *The Philosophy of the Enlightenment* (Princeton, 1951 ; orig. German ed. 1932), though much praised, treats ideas too schematically, and without adequate reference to context or chronology. On a larger scale, P. Gay, *The Enlightenment: An Interpretation*, 2 vols (London, 1966–9), is a rich source of bibliographical information about the period, as well as in part a reply to L. G. Crocker, *The Age of Crisis*, 2 vols (Baltimore, 1959–63), which has been criticized for dwelling too much on the negative aspects of eighteenth-century thought, but nevertheless points up well the period's fundamental dilemmas.

In default of a good general work on seventeenth-century thought, there is much to be said for beginning by reading Aldous Huxley, *The Devils of Loudun* (London, 1952), both as a reminder that not everything in the intellectual history of the period is to be accounted for in terms of the rise of scientific rationalism, and for its penetrating insight into what the author rightly calls 'that strange agglomeration of incongruities, the seventeenth-century mind'. Following this, there are various ways of investigating the changing attitudes which led to the eventual dominance of rationalism. Chronologically, one would begin with the sixteenth-century Italian sources whose background is well explained by P. O. Kristeller, *Renaissance Thought: the Classic, Scholastic, and Humanistic Strains* (New York, 1961), and then go on to the influences that undermined traditional modes of thought, discussed by R. H. Popkin, *A History of Scepticism from Erasmus to Descartes*, rev. ed. (The Hague, 1964), before coming to J. S. Spink, *French Free-Thought from Gassendi to Voltaire* (London, 1960), an altogether indispensable account of the development of naturalism and rationalism in the period. Among the major authors met with in Spink's earlier pages, Cyrano de Bergerac should be read in H. Weber's edition of *L'Autre Monde* (Paris, 1958), because of its excellent introduction. R. Lenoble, *Mersenne ou la naissance du mécanisme* (Paris, 1943), analyses many relatively inaccessible texts, while the symposium *Pierre Gassendi, sa vie et son œuvre* (Paris, 1955) is a good way of approaching another author whose actual works are hard to come by. There is also a specialist study, O. R. Bloch, *La Philosophie de Gassendi* (The Hague, 1971). The culminating point of Popkin's book, and the nodal point of Spink's, is Descartes. L. Roth, *Descartes' Discourse on Method* (Oxford, 1937), can still be read with profit, but the best introduction is A. Kenny, *Descartes, a Study of his Philosophy* (New York, 1968), and the best short account in French is F. Alquié, *Descartes, l'homme et l'œuvre* (Paris, 1956).

A lively introduction to the writings of the *libertins* is to be had from A. Adam, *Les Libertins* (Paris, 1964), an anthology of extracts. The relationships between the 'libertins érudits', as well as their ideas, are exhaustively studied by R. Pintard, *Le Libertinage érudit pendant la première moitié du dix-septième siècle* (Paris, 1943). Like H. Busson in his wider-ranging but more discursive *La Pensée religieuse française de Charron à Pascal* (Paris, 1933) and *La Religion des classiques* (Paris, 1948), Pintard sees these authors as deliberately bent on the subversion of religious faith. The same tendency marks the celebrated work of P. Hazard, *La Crise de la conscience européenne*, 3 vols (Paris, 1934; subsequently publ. in one vol. without notes and references), an extremely readable but, in the light of later work (much of it inspired by Hazard himself), somewhat superficial account of the mutation of the religious values of the seventeenth century into the secular humanism of the eighteenth. The reaction, in which the thinkers in question are seen as authentic if heterodox Christians, has probably gone too far, for the issues were in fact never so sharply drawn between genuine belief and subversive intent. It has, however, brought important gains, particularly in the case of Bayle. E. Labrousse, *Pierre Bayle* (The Hague, 1963–4), is a monumental work; the second volume, *Hétérodoxie et rigorisme*, convincingly rescues Bayle from the charge of complete scepticism and stresses the positive aspects of his thought, while W. Rex, *Pierre Bayle and Religious Controversy* (The Hague, 1965), puts beyond doubt the importance of Bayle's Calvinist background for a true understanding of his ideas. Another important work is C. B. Brush, *Montaigne and Bayle: Variations on the Theme of Scepticism* (The Hague, 1966), which also usefully complements Popkin's *History of Scepticism* already cited. In view of the comparative inaccessibility of Bayle's *Dictionnaire* outside the major libraries, it is worth noting that Popkin and Brush have edited a volume of selections in English translation (New York, 1965) and that one in French is promised (by A. Niderst). With the other major thinker of the 'crise', Fontenelle, the problem concerns not so much his religious position as his scientific stance. There is an excellent short introduction to his ideas in M.

Bouchard, *L' 'Histoire des Oracles' de Fontenelle* (Paris, 1947), which goes well beyond the promise of its title. J. R. Carré, *La Philosophie de Fontenelle, ou le sourire de la raison* (Paris, 1932), is a work by a philosopher which takes no account of (indeed it denies) any development in Fontenelle's thought. It should be complemented and where necessary corrected by A. Niderst, *Fontenelle à la recherche de lui-même (1657–1702)* (Paris, 1972), which adopts the historical method (and is of interest beyond the terminal date indicated in its title). On the problematical issue of Fontenelle's position in the dispute between Cartesians and Newtonians, on which Niderst has some good pages, there is a valuable and original discussion in L. Marsak, *Fontenelle and the idea of science in the French Enlightenment* (Philadelphia, 1959), and many important references in Ehrard's *L'Idée de nature* . . . praised at the beginning of this bibliography.

On the ethical thought of the period under review, there is no lack of books describing the attitudes of the more celebrated 'moralistes' of the seventeenth century. The two most stimulating are P. Bénichou, *Morales du grand siècle* (Paris, 1948), and A. J. Krailsheimer, *Studies in Self-Interest from Descartes to La Bruyère* (Oxford, 1962). The 'moralistes' were largely concerned with contemporary life styles, but there was also an abundant literature which dealt with moral philosophy of a more technical kind. Here, the book by A. Levi, *French Moralists and Theories of the Passions, 1585–1649* (Oxford, 1964), is fundamental, but those who find it hard going might do well to seek out the long article by J. E. D'Angers, 'Le Renouveau du stoïcisme au XVIe et au XVIIe siècles' in the proceedings of the Seventh International Congress of the Association Guillaume Budé published at Paris in 1964, which will help to break the back of the subject.

The origins of Jansenism are steadily being laid bare in a series of monographs under the direction of J. Orcibal. Meanwhile L. Cognet, *Le Jansénisme* (Paris, 1961), gives a succinct account of its history, and G. Delassault, *La Pensée janséniste en dehors de Pascal* (Paris, 1963), a useful introduction to some of its less well-known figures. The interpretation of Jansenism continues to be controversial, the more so since the Jansenists differed widely amongst themselves on many points. An excellent comparison of the Jansenist and Jesuit standpoints is to be found in R. R. Palmer, *Catholics and Unbelievers in 18th Century France* (New York, 1961). In the eighteenth century itself, Jansenism was more important from a political than from a doctrinal point of view, as can be seen from L. Taveneaux, *Jansénisme et politique* (Paris, 1965), which includes an anthology of texts. The (somewhat paradoxical) relationship between some Jansenist ideas and those of the Enlightenment is among the topics investigated by E. D. James, *Pierre Nicole, Jansenist and Humanist* (The Hague, 1972).

Work on Pascal, of course, often casts light on Jansenism. Here J. Miel, *Pascal and Theology* (Baltimore, 1969), and P. Sellier, *Pascal et Saint Augustin* (Paris, 1970), are noteworthy. Both books also give the lie to those who have held that Pascal was not competent to write on theological matters. The best short guide to Pascal is J. Mesnard, *Pascal, l'homme et l'œuvre* (Paris, 1952). The symposium *Pascal présent* (Clermont-Ferrand, 1962) contains valuable articles by R. Pintard and H. Gouhier exploring the relationship between Pascal's ideas and contemporary free-thought. The historically important text of the Port-Royal edition of the *Pensées* has been republished in a critical edition by G. Couton and J. Jehasse (Paris, 1971). In general, however, the student should use the text established by

L. Lafuma, which supplants all previous versions; it is most conveniently to be found, along with Pascal's *Lettres provinciales* and other major writings, in the 'Intégrale' edition (Paris, 1963).

The transformation of moral ideas at the end of the seventeenth century and the beginning of the eighteenth is studied by R. Mauzi, *L'Idée du bonheur au 18e siècle* (Paris, 1960). The same work also underlines the shift from an other-worldly to a this-worldly attitude to human existence, which caused many Catholic apologists of the period to give hostages to secularism. The orthodoxy of Bossuet and the conflicts into which it led him is illuminated by T. Goyet, *L'Humanisme de Bossuet* (Paris, 1965), and by J. Truchet, *La Prédication de Bossuet*, 2 vols (Paris, 1960). On his political ideas, J. Truchet, *Politique de Bossuet* (Paris, 1966), is a useful commentated anthology. For Fénelon's political ideas, see C. Urbain's edition of *Écrits et lettres politiques* (Paris, 1920). Fénelon's clash with Bossuet over quietism, and his political views, make him one of the most interesting figures of his period, but there is no good short introduction to his thought. J. L. Goré, *L'Itinéraire de Fénelon* (Paris, 1957), is excellent but very long. Nor is there yet a reliable monograph on Saint-Évremond.

The influence of Descartes pervades the latter part of the seventeenth century, as that of the rationalist thinkers whom he influenced does the beginning of the eighteenth. F. Bouillier, *Histoire de la philosophie cartésienne*, 2 vols (Paris, 1868), is still useful, although it has been superseded on many points, notably by Spink in his chapter 'The Fortunes of Descartes'. An important Cartesian topic has been investigated by L. C. Rosenfield, *From Beast-Machine to Man-Machine* (New York, 1941), and H. Kirkinen, *Les Origines de la conception moderne de l'homme machine* (Helsinki, 1960). That Cartesianism was not identical with the philosophy of Descartes is one of the points well made by G. Rodis-Lewis, *Descartes et le rationalisme*, 'Que sais-je' series (Paris, 1966). Mme Rodis-Lewis discusses Malebranche, Spinoza and Leibniz, all of whom were highly influential in France. Her own *Nicolas Malebranche* (Paris, 1963) is also recommended. The extent of Spinoza's influence is shown by P. Vernière, *Spinoza et la pensée française avant la Révolution*, 2 vols (Paris, 1954) (cf. also J. Moreau, *Spinoza et le spinozisme*, 'Que sais-je?' series (Paris, 1971)), and that of Leibniz by W. H. Barber, *Leibniz in France from Arnauld to Voltaire* (Oxford, 1955).

The influence of thinkers who were mainly outside the Cartesian orbit is also important when we come to assess the ideas of the early *philosophes*. Fénelon's influence is considered by A. Chérel, *Fénelon en France au 18e siècle* (Paris, 1917), and Bayle's by P. Retat, *Le Dictionnaire de Bayle et la lutte philosophique au 18e siècle* (Paris, 1971), and by H. T. Mason, *Pierre Bayle and Voltaire* (Oxford, 1963). Foreign influences are treated by N. L. Torrey, *Voltaire and the English Deists* (New Haven, 1930), and by D. Schlegel, *Shaftesbury and the French Deists* (Chapel Hill, 1956). A thorough study of Locke's influence in France remains to be written. On the *philosophes* themselves, an excellent introduction is provided by A. Adam, *Le Mouvement philosophique dans la première moitié du 18e siècle* (Paris, 1967), which includes a concise survey of social and political conditions, and of major philosophical themes. On Montesquieu, R. Shackleton, *Montesquieu, a Critical Biography* (Oxford, 1961), is the authoritative work. G. Lanson, *Voltaire* (Paris, 1906), and R. Naves, *Voltaire, l'homme et l'œuvre* (Paris, 1942), have held their value, but the essential study is R. Pomeau, *La Religion de Voltaire* (Paris, 1956), which traces

Voltaire's intellectual development in masterly fashion and brings out clearly the extent and depth of his fundamental deism.

Pomeau has an excellent chapter on Voltaire and the materialists, whose thought is now being given something like its due by scholars. Here the most important books are that by Ehrard already praised, and J. Roger, *Les Sciences de la vie dans la pensée française du 18e siècle* (Paris, 1963), which between them have revolutionized scholarly perspectives on eighteenth-century French thought. Also stimulating is A. Vartanian, *Diderot and Descartes* (Princeton, 1953), although it overstresses the role of Cartesianism in the formation of late eighteenth-century materialism, and a more apt title for it would have been 'From Descartes to Diderot'. One way of gaining immediate access to the ideas of the materialists is to read the remarkable introduction by J. Varloot to his edition of Diderot, *Le Rêve de d'Alembert* (Paris, 1971), followed by the texts and introduction in R. Desné, *Les Matérialistes français de 1750 à 1800* (Paris, 1965). A good range of materialist texts (often, however, in the form of excerpts) is published by Les Éditions Sociales of Paris.

Diderot's capital place in the development of materialist thought is well appreciated by Varloot in the introduction just mentioned. Intimations of materialism in his contributions to the *Encyclopédie* are highlighted by J. Proust not only in *Diderot et l'Encyclopédie* (Paris, 1962), but also in the shorter *L'Encyclopédie* (Paris, 1965) which stands with J. Lough, *The Encyclopédie* (London, 1971), as the best account of the whole undertaking. Diderot's own thought is best approached by way of J. Thomas, *L'Humanisme de Diderot*, 2nd ed. (Paris, 1938), which has stood the test of time well despite the subsequent discovery of important new material; H. Dieckmann, *Cinq leçons sur Diderot* (Geneva, 1959); and the valuable chapters in J. Fabre, *Lumières et romantisme* (Paris, 1963), and Niklaus's *Literary History* already mentioned.

The best approach to Rousseau is through the Pléiade edition of his *Œuvres complètes* (Paris, 1959–   ); among the excellent introductions by well-known scholars, that by M. Raymond to the *Rêveries* is outstanding. Rousseau has been called an individualist and a collectivist, a rationalist and a man of feeling. These to some degree unavoidable dichotomies are well dealt with by E. Cassirer, *The Question of Jean-Jacques Rousseau*, trans. P. Gay (New York, 1954; original German ed. 1932), by P. Gay, *The Party of Humanity* (London, 1964), and especially by J. McManners, *The Social Contract and Rousseau's Revolt against Society* (Leicester, 1968) – this short lecture, with its mine of bibliographical information in the notes as well as its stimulating argument, provides a most useful introduction to Rousseau's thought. A fuller, more expository guide is to be found in J. H. Broome, *Rousseau, a Study of his Thought* (London, 1963). R. Derathé, *Jean-Jacques Rousseau et la science politique de son temps* (Paris, 1950), is fundamental. P. M. Masson, *La Religion de Rousseau*, 3 vols (Paris, 1916), contains much that is valuable but badly overstresses Rousseau's 'emotionalism'. The best examination of Rousseau's philosophy as an expression of his personality is P. Burgelin, *La Philosophie de l'existence de Jean-Jacques Rousseau* (Paris, 1952). The vagaries of some Rousseau criticism show how much work still needs to be done on the notion of 'sensibilité' in the eighteenth century. R. Mortier, *Clartés et ombres du siècle des lumières* (Paris, 1969), argues cogently against splitting the period chronologically into an 'age of reason' followed by an 'age of sensibility', as also does Gay in *The Party of Humanity*. Mortier's book also contains a fascinating account of the history of the idea of 'les lumières' in the period.

With the approach of the Revolution, French eighteenth-century thought begins to resemble that 'agglomeration of incongruities' which Huxley found at the beginning of the previous century. Evidence of this is to be found in R. Darnton, *Mesmerism and the End of the Enlightenment in France* (New York, 1969), and in the classic work of A. Viatte, *Les Sources occultes du romantisme français*, 2 vols (Paris, 1928). The contribution of the *philosophes* to the Revolution is still controversial. On the role of the *idéologues*, there is a book by C. H. Van Duzer, *The Contribution of the Idéologues to the French Revolution* (Baltimore, 1933), but their actual ideas are perhaps best approached through the now rather old book by R. Picavet, *Les Idéologues* (Paris, 1891), and the writings of Cabanis, whose *Rapports* . . . is included in Vol. 1 of the edition of his *Œuvres philosophiques* by C. Lehec and J. Cazeneuve (Paris, 1956).

In addition to the works mentioned in this essay, many valuable contributions are to be found in the specialist periodicals and series of monographs in which work on the subject is constantly being brought up to date. Mention may be made in particular of *Dix-septième siècle*, *Dix-huitième siècle* and the volumes of *Studies on Voltaire and the 18th Century*, *Diderot Studies* and *Annales de la Société Jean-Jacques Rousseau*.

FRENCH THOUGHT IN THE NINETEENTH AND TWENTIETH CENTURIES

D. G. *Charlton*

Introduction – the Intellectual Context

French thought in the nineteenth century was marked first and fore-most by intensified complexity and conflict. Certainly the preoccupa-tions of the pre-revolutionary period persisted into the new age. On the one hand, the conservative orthodoxy of Catholicism continued to be defended and was restated even more firmly by such Traditional-ist thinkers as Joseph de Maistre, Bonald and Lamennais (and, more lyrically, in Chateaubriand's *Le Génie du christianisme*). On the other hand, the empirically minded, agnostic, reforming tradition of Vol-taire and the *philosophes* was maintained by *idéologues* like Destutt de Tracy and Cabanis and was extended – dramatically so – by the posi-tivists from Henri de Saint-Simon and Auguste Comte to Littré, Renan, Taine and others in the later years of the century, and by socialistic reformers such as the Saint-Simonians, Fourier, Étienne Cabet, Pierre Leroux, Proudhon and Louis Blanc. Even the Eclectic group of thinkers, led by Victor Cousin and including Laromiguière, Royer-Collard and Jouffroy, was continuing the eighteenth-century search for a natural religion and a natural ethic, as it elaborated a middle way between the religious approach of the Catholics and the scientific and reforming approach of the *idéologues*, positivists and socialists. Yet the undeniable continuities were all but submerged by the changes – social and economic, educational and institutional, amongst others – ushered in by the Revolution and its aftermath. Thus, for example, the horrors of the Terror appeared to many observers in the new century to have stemmed from unbelief in France – 'Société sans dieu, qui par Dieu fus frappée', as Hugo was typical in asserting. Both conservatives and reformers assumed that ideas govern history, that political order can only be built upon philosophical order, and consequently the yearning for a more stable society transmitted to philosophical dispute a sense of urgent, practical significance. Moreover the harsh economic and social consequences of the industrial revolution in France reinforced the sense of crisis, for society as well as for the individual, attached to debates that were in part old and yet were now renewed by the differences of context and historical moment. Further-more, the issues were intrinsically major and far-reaching – science and religion, free will and determinism, history and progress, economic *laissez-faire* and the new socialism, social conservation and social revolution – and it is thus no wonder that this generation should have felt it lived at a turning-point in history and ideas alike, in an age of revolutions that were intellectual no less than political and economic. In this situation some felt saddened by uncertainty and doubt – like the deeply liberal Quinet when he declared that 'aujourd'hui le monde entier est le grand sépulcre où toutes les croyances, comme toutes les espérances, semblent pour jamais ensevelies' (or like Stendhal's Bishop of Besançon in *Le Rouge et le noir* as he evokes 'cet état d'inquiétude et de doute qui, au dix-neuvième siècle, désole des esprits tristes et ennuyés'). Others were daunted and yet more hopeful – like such Romantics as Hugo and George Sand or Lamennais in his later years when he observed:

Le vieux monde se dissout, les vieilles doctrines s'éteignent; mais, au milieu d'un travail confus, d'un désordre apparent, on voit poindre des doctrines nouvelles, s'organiser un monde nouveau ...

Yet others such as Saint-Simon and Comte were transparently confi-dent, sure that their own doctrine had arrived on its crucial historical cue and was uniquely fitted to rise to the level of the times.

The expansion and reform of higher education under Napoleon and the Restoration monarchy added to the argumentative confusion. The number of academic posts in philosophy, history, science and other disciplines was steadily increasing; unlike almost every major French thinker prior to 1789, their nineteenth-century successors commonly held university chairs. As to philosophy itself, under measures taken from the 1830s onwards by a philosopher-administrator like Victor Cousin, it almost pre-empted the role in the French educational curri-culum that had belonged to religion. Effectively, society was subsidizing intellectual controversy, and consequently philosophical activity both increased and became far more professional – perhaps not with wholly beneficial results, for many nineteenth-century works of philosophy lack lucidity in both content and style. And another important factor that encouraged franker debate was the gradual extension of intellectual freedom; though there were certainly moments of panic-stricken repression, toleration was much increased over the century, and freedom to publish led naturally to a still larger diversity of ideas.

The nineteenth century was also a time – throughout Europe – of rapidly widening knowledge, and philosophical, religious and social thought was immensely affected by new facts, arguments and theories drawn from the natural sciences, from historical and philological studies and (by the mid-century) from the new 'human sciences' of sociology and psychology. A first example is offered by the renewal of studies in the history of philosophy. The ideas of earlier and of contemporary foreign thinkers were perhaps more widely diffused than at any time since the Renaissance – first by Madame de Staël and Constant, then Cousin and his Eclectic group, Quinet and Michelet (both much affected by current German learning), and many others throughout the century. Spinoza, Kant, Herder, Hegel, Schopenhauer, Feuerbach, Hartmann; Mill, Carlyle, Spencer, Darwin: these are only the most influential of the foreign writers who were admired, attacked and invoked, often in somewhat partial interpretations, and whose thought served to renew old arguments and to prompt new syntheses.

Even more decisive in some ways was the expansion of the natural sciences. From the creation of the École Polytechnique in 1794 and the re-establishment of the Académie des Sciences in 1795 onwards French science gained an international authority with physicists like Ampère and Sadi Carnot, chemists like Gay-Lussac, and biologists such as Lamarck, Geoffroy Saint-Hilaire and Cuvier, and the second half of the century saw Berthelot's creation of thermochemistry, Pasteur's foundation of bacteriology and fermentation science, Claude Bernard's pioneering studies on the liver and autonomic nervous system, and Henri Becquerel's work on the radioactivity of uranium. Moreover, whereas eighteenth-century science was only familiar to an educated minority, in the new era the power of science was clear to everyone through its everyday applications – in much improved surgery and medicine, in gas lighting, in industrialization and the railways.

This 'scientific revolution', as it has been fairly described, had vast intellectual repercussions, and so also did the concurrent expansion of historical and philological studies that was encouraged by both

Napoleon and later Governments, which created chairs of history in every university and in a variety of practical ways promoted scholarly research. Renan rightly refers to the 'revolution' (the same recurrent word) 'qui depuis 1820 a changé complètement la face des études historiques'. Some scholars were above all narrative historians – Thierry and Fustel de Coulanges, for example; others, such as Guizot, Michelet and Tocqueville, had a more theoretical interest in French or European history and studied historical developments in order to discern their underlying causes and phases; yet others, like Quinet, were above all philosophers of history, deriving from the examination of man's past a variety of theories concerning human progress and decadence. And not least important (and intellectually disruptive in their quiet, erudite way) were the *philologues*, probing into the remoter past, discovering more of the civilizations of Greece, Rome, India, China and elsewhere and of Nordic, Celtic and Romance folklore. Fostered by the foundation in 1795 of the École des Langues Orientales Vivantes and inspired by the example of distinguished German scholars such as Creuzer and Görres, French philology – by which was meant not only the mainly linguistic study of our own time but a much wider study of the history of the human spirit over the ages, centred in particular on the history of religions – made striking advances over the century. Through the many translations of ancient texts and the studies of ancient cultures by orientalists like Eugène Burnouf (a major mediator of Buddhist thought) and of hellenists like Louis Ménard, friend of Leconte de Lisle, French thought and literature alike were enriched by what Quinet called '[une] Renaissance orientale'. And as with the sciences and the history of philosophy, so too this influx of new ideas about history deeply affected the thinkers of the day. Some found in history a new creed based on the idea of progress, whilst others tried to rejuvenate the religions of antiquity and the alleged insights of primitive mythologies. Yet others attempted to denigrate Christianity by comparing it with other faiths, either to show that all share the same superstitions or that earlier ethics are superior to Christian morality, and still others were to draw from their survey of the history of civilizations a pessimistic doctrine of the inevitable decline and fall of all human societies. And – perhaps the most explosive of the *philologues'* contentions – Christianity was challenged to withstand the same dispassionate historical scrutiny as was applied to other creeds.

For all these reasons therefore, and for others, this chapter concerns a period of marked intellectual upheaval no less than of political,

economic and social upheaval, a time of fierce ideological conflict leading to an ever extremer polarization of attitudes as between Catholics
and freethinkers, spiritualists and materialists, right-wing conservatives
and left-wing reformers and socialists. Any selective survey will thus
inevitably oversimplify; it can at best seek to sketch certain major trends
and isolate – even if misleadingly at times – some salient areas of controversy. The bibliography indicates guides to the history of philosophy in the more technical, professional sense; this chapter itself
attempts to evoke the intellectual history of the time in more general
terms, as it impinged upon a far wider public than the philosophers
themselves.

It is rash to indicate any single theme underlying this survey: for the
reasons suggested above all is complexity. But if such a theme can be
found, it perhaps lies in the continuing tension between the scientific
humanism of *idéologues*, positivists and others and the spiritualistic and
often explicitly religious humanism of Catholics, idealist philosophers
and others. In the earlier part of our period the initiative seemed to lie
above all with the former outlook: Christianity was under attack; the
scientific method was triumphantly extended to include the 'human
sciences'; this was an 'age of systems', a time when new creeds in place
of the old were widely propounded. The later years of the period,
from around 1870 onwards, witnessed a strong critical reaction to these
systems and creeds, a striking revival of Catholic thought, and – through
the impact of Bergson in particular – a broadly diffused renewal of the
idealist tradition in French philosophy. Clearly, such a schema greatly
simplifies: in the earlier years, for example, Catholics, Eclectics and a
philosopher like Maine de Biran were fighting against the new
positivism; in the later years positivists like Durkheim and Lévy-Bruhl
were still more influential than their predecessors, and Marxism, be-
longing to the same general tradition, has remained a major pro-
tagonist in present-day conflicts. Yet – treated with every caution – it
may provide a preliminary orientation.

Science and the Rise of Positivism

The nineteenth century was pre-eminently the time when scientific
humanism came of age as a fully argued philosophy – thanks, first, to
the *idéologue* group, but more emphatically to the positivists who continued and extended its scientific approach.

The rise of positivism had two sources above all. The first was the 'scientific revolution' already outlined: its immense achievements naturally fostered an enthusiastic confidence in science and even a belief that scientific knowledge alone is reliable. Some – including such scientists as Cuvier, Ampère and Pasteur – might protest that there are moral and spiritual truths beyond the reach of the scientific method, but far more – including such men of letters as Hugo and Zola – were persuaded that science held out an unlimited future of material progress and human happiness. Secondly, the positivist philosophers inherited the empiricist tradition of the eighteenth century and earlier. From Bacon in England and Gassendi in France onwards an increasing number of thinkers had argued that knowledge is most reliably – or, indeed, uniquely – to be gained by deduction from what we observe. Descartes and other rationalist philosophers had contended, on the other hand, that we can attain *a priori* knowledge, prior to sense-experience; for Descartes the model was mathematics, and just as one can progress from the axioms of Euclid to other truths in geometry, so in other areas, he argued, reason can work from 'innate ideas' or from allegedly self-evident truths such as the existence of the self to arrive at other truths, especially in the realm of metaphysics. By contrast, the empiricists – Locke, Hume and others in England, and Fontenelle, *philosophes* like Condillac, Helvétius and others in France – took as their model branch of knowledge the science of physics, impressed above all by the discoveries of Newton. Man is born without 'innate ideas', a blank sheet, and all he can know must be *a posteriori*, after sense-experience (with the sole exceptions of the tautologous truths of mathematical and logical systems). 'Nothing in the mind which was not first in the senses'; 'nous n'avons point d'idées qui ne nous viennent des sens', in Condillac's words – such is the empiricist view and the basis of positivism, the theory of knowledge which the nineteenth-century positivists explored and expanded.

The first to do so was Henri de Saint-Simon (1760–1825). After a career as a soldier fighting with the Americans in the War of Independence and as a financial speculator, he became persuaded in middle age that his true mission was as an intellectual called to establish a new philosophy as the essential foundation for a new social reconstruction. Though influenced strongly by the *philosophes*, he claimed that their work was largely critical and that a positive system must be created in place of the Christian creed they had destroyed. And from his early writings – such as the *Introduction aux travaux scientifiques du dix-neuvième siècle* (1807–8) and his *Mémoire sur la science de l'homme* (1813) – onwards he asserted, as these titles imply, that the future lies with the sciences. Not only must they be unified and given a systematic theoretical basis; above all, the scientific method must be extended to man and human society, and this new 'science de l'homme' will rapidly lead to a scientific reorganization of society, to be hastened by giving far greater political authority to scientists and especially to the new 'social scientists'. In economic affairs likewise power should be given to the well-informed; he anticipated both socialism and a belief in what has since been called 'the managerial revolution' and urged that the workers and the managers – industrialists, bankers and the like – should unite (against such parasites as kings, aristocrats and soldiers, who draw on a wealth they do nothing to create) to enforce a more just and effective system of production and distribution – views which led Marx and Engels to praise him as 'with Hegel, the most encyclopedic mind of his age'. He differed from the socialists later in that he denied that there is any necessary clash of interests between the capitalists and the workers and he also defended the right to private property where it is used for the benefit of society as a whole, but he can rightly be seen as a major precursor of socialism in his demand that social and economic affairs should be planned by the State for the physical, mental and moral well-being of 'la classe la plus nombreuse et la plus pauvre'. Nor did Saint-Simon neglect the importance of religion as a moral spur and a unifying 'spiritual power', and he therefore sketched a new creed to replace Christianity and what he believed its socially reactionary and other-worldly attitudes. This was originally to have been a purely scientific and even materialistic system, enshrining Newton as religious prophet, but in his final years he developed the ideas of his *Nouveau Christianisme* (1825). Here he strongly criticized both Catholics and Protestants and claimed that Christ's own essential teaching is a gospel of charity and fraternity:

> Dieu a dit: *Les hommes doivent se conduire en frères à l'égard les uns des autres;* ce principe sublime renferme tout ce qu'il y a de divin dans la religion chrétienne.

The 'golden age', he asserted, does not lie in the past, in the Garden of Eden, or in a future life in heaven, but in an imminent earthly future when social order and fraternity have been established. Saint-Simon did not live to elaborate the teaching, worship and organization of the new Christian Church, and it was thus left to such disciples as Enfantin and Bazard to start churches and even a religious community and to develop the doctrines of the Saint-Simonian religion in the form which was to attract, amongst many others, the writers of the *Jung Deutschland* movement and several of the French Romantics. Indeed, the very varied theories of this warm-hearted and almost too fertile social thinker were to be widely influential – in the development of socialist ideas; in economic action under Louis-Napoléon; even in the building of the Suez and Panama Canals. And in philosophy likewise he provided the general ideas that others would restate in a more detailed and forceful way.

Chief amongst these thinkers was Auguste Comte (1798–1857), who began his career as secretary to Saint-Simon, and whilst the extent of his own originality can be debated, it is hard to deny that Comte gave the positivist philosophy its fullest exposition – to the point that he is commonly considered its intellectual 'father'.

Comte's work, pursued with relentless devotion from the age of nineteen, when he joined Saint-Simon, until his death, can be divided into two parts. In the first, best represented by his *Cours de philosophie positive* (1830–42), his concerns were with philosophy and the establishment of social science: this was the work which affected Littré and John Stuart Mill so profoundly and, after Harriet Martineau's abridged translation of the *Cours* in 1853, English writers such as Frederic Harrison, G. H. Lewes and George Eliot. In later life, after a short but intense relation with Clotilde de Vaux, he turned much more to social ethics and especially the creation of a new 'religion of humanity', which he expounded in works like his *Système de politique positive* (1851–4) and *Le Catéchisme positiviste* (1852). Now, he claimed, having already transformed science into philosophy, he would – a new St Paul – transform philosophy into religion. We shall observe this attempt later; here we are concerned with his earlier expression of his 'positive philosophy'.

Comte's central purpose was to establish a philosophy of science that would provide the basis for a scientific reordering of society. In the very first *leçon* of the *Cours* he announced his discovery of 'une grande loi fondamentale' governing the development of the human mind throughout history – his famous 'loi des trois états'. In every department of thought and life man moves in turn from the 'theological' to the 'metaphysical' and finally to the 'scientific, or positive' state. The theological mode of thinking assumes that we can attain an 'absolute' knowledge of the first or ultimate causes of events. In particular it attributes final causal power to one or more 'supernatural agents' whose intervention explains many of the occurrences within the natural order – thunder, for instance, being the expression of the anger of the gods and plague a divine punishment for sin. This 'state' also determines men's thought about their own life and society; thus, for example, the ruler within society and the husband within the family are conceived of as godlike, authoritarian figures. The second, metaphysical, state – which supervened in Europe from the time of the Renaissance – is a modification of the first. Men still believe they can know first causes and attain an absolute knowledge of ultimate reality, but now causal explanations are in terms of 'abstract forces' instead of 'supernatural agents'. The special error of this phase, Comte argues, is to attribute independent existence and power to our own abstractions, whether notions in science like 'the ether' or metaphysical concepts like 'nature'. Gradually, however, in at least some areas men's minds have advanced to the third state, 'l'état positif'. Men now recognize the impossibility of absolute knowledge, of the search for first and final causes, and by relying on observation combined with reasoning they concentrate on discovering the 'effective laws' determining the world of phenomena. This scientific approach, renouncing all theological or metaphysical explanations, has largely triumphed in the natural sciences, Comte continues: thus, astrology has given way to astronomy, alchemy to chemistry, and so on. But it must now be extended to the study of man and society – through the progress of physiology and above all through a new science – sociology – 'la physique sociale'. To establish this one missing science is, he says in the *Cours*, 'le plus grand et le plus pressant besoin de notre intelligence' and 'le premier but de ce cours, son but spécial'. Only by becoming fully scientific will the study of society be able to predict future phenomena, like the other sciences do, and thereafter adopt suitable social policies. 'Science, d'où prévoyance; prévoyance, d'où action': this was his motto from the start and remained his dominant concern as in turn he provided an allegedly historical demonstration of the truth of the 'loi des trois états', as he examined the methods of the various sciences in order to identify the theological and metaphysical errors still persisting in them, as he classified the sciences in their proper order, moving from the most simple to the most complex (and most useful to man) – mathematics, astronomy, physics, chemistry, biology, sociology – and as, above all, he discussed the methodology of social science. Observation is its basic method, though he fears this may be mere sterile 'empiricism' unless directed by some hypothesis one wishes to verify; experimentation is also possible in so far as we can note what happens in a society when some special factor, like a revolution, interferes with its normal functioning; and comparison is another fruitful method – between human and animal societies and between coexisting human societies. But above all he looks to a new method, peculiar to sociology: the historical method. By studying the history of societies up to the present we can verify the laws of 'social statics', of the factors that keep societies relatively stable, and discover the laws of 'social dynamics' – the factors producing change, the tendencies that have grown stronger and will become dominant in the future.

Such were the main ideas that earned him the status of a 'founder' of sociology and which led Mill and others to describe him as 'one of the principal thinkers of the age'. Yet it is not only his later religious teachings which may be thought to go beyond the limits of the positivist theory of knowledge from which he began. In his haste to reorder society and because of his rather dogmatic *esprit de système* he tends in this direction even in the *Cours*. In the first place, one may suggest, he was all too often uncritical and unscientific in his attitude to facts and has fairly been accused of selecting the facts which supported his generalizations and ignoring those which did not, especially in his treatment of history. Secondly, his theories rested upon certain assumptions which he failed to justify – that ideas determine history, for example, or that each stage in the evolution of mankind is rigidly determined and inevitable – and he never demonstrated that his laws were more than a pattern he was imposing on history or, alternatively, that they were validated by their predictive success. And above all perhaps he took it for granted that sociology can in fact be fully scientific. Early in the *Cours* his claims for it were relatively modest and he admitted that its methods were imperfect, but by the end he was attributing to it 'autant de positivité et plus de rationalité qu'aucune des sciences antérieures déjà jugées par ce Traité'. His reduction of historical change to a few dominant laws, the dogmatism of his social theories, and the authoritarian organization he later devised for his religion – which he claimed to be no less scientific – were all symptoms of his 'scientism' – an exaggeration of the positivist position that greatly overrates both the potential range of science and the degree of certainty to which its conclusions can lay claim. Thereby he illustrates one of the most significant developments in nineteenth-century French thought – the move, in positivistic thinkers, towards an extreme confidence that science can solve all mysteries and answer all questions with assured authority.

Other positivists illustrated the same tendency, but directed to different ends, and none more so than Taine during the later part of the century. Hippolyte Taine (1828–93) lost his Christian faith as a youth and rapidly moved to a positivist outlook under the influence of the *idéologues*. He achieved repute in a surprisingly broad range of subjects – in literary history with his studies of La Fontaine (1853), Livy (1856) and his celebrated *Histoire de la littérature anglaise* (1864); in philosophical polemics with *Les Philosophes classiques du dix-neuvième siècle en France* (1857), an attack upon the unscientific philosophy of the Eclectics; in art history, in which he was professor at the École des Beaux-Arts from 1864; in psychology with *De l'intelligence* (1870); and in history with his vast and controversial work on *Les Origines de la France contemporaine* (1875–93). But underlying this diversity there was a unity of aim – to explore human psychology, either directly or as expressed in literature, art and historical action – and a unity of method, for in all these areas he sought to justify and apply a single, universal approach based in the first place on the positivist theory. He appeared to many of his contemporaries as the embodiment of scientific humanism in its most high-minded and uncompromising form. Thus, for example, he stood alongside Théodule Ribot and Pierre Janet as a champion of scientific psychology, and even if much of *De l'intelligence* may now be outdated, it helped to replace the previous reliance on mere introspection (as exemplified by the Eclectics) by an emphasis on experiment, the search for causes, the physiological basis of personality and the study of pathological cases – though this attitude not surprisingly intensified his opponents' accusations of materialistic determinism. Even literature, and especially the novel, he urged, should be a 'collection of experiments', a contribution to a scientific understanding of human nature, revealing the physical and psychological determinants of man's behaviour – a view accepted by literary admirers like Flaubert, Zola and Maupassant. 'Toute réalité est perçue expérimentalement par l'homme', he asserted – a view which led him to reject the ideas of God, the supernatural, the soul, and its immortality. He even contended, most notoriously, that our moral decisions are as causally determined as any other natural event: 'le vice et la vertu sont des produits comme le vitriol et le sucre' – albeit he argued that moral responsibility remained compatible with determinism as he conceived it. He brought a similar attitude to his study of literature and art, and his method was well stated in the celebrated Introduction to his *Histoire de la littérature anglaise* in which he gave his ambitious and stimulating ideas for the future of a 'scientific' cultural history, a study which he believed could lead us to discern the great causal factors operating in history as a whole. Examination of the literary 'documents' will lead us to a deeper understanding of their author's psychology, and this, complemented by scrutiny of the facts of his life and personality, will in turn permit us to grasp the 'faculté-maîtresse' – the disposition of thought and feeling – which determines his work. And we can then go further still and 'explain' this by reference to three great 'causal facts', the author's 'race', 'milieu' and 'moment' – that is, in brief, his inherited personality, the social, political and geographical background, and the historical context in which he was writing. Even now, however, Taine's ambitions are not exhausted, for he maintains that the same three factors underlie all historical phenomena and that the historian can thus discover the laws of history and observe their operation in the main provinces of human civilization – religion, art, philosophy, government, the family and industry. His bold claim here is thus that a literary document, scientifically studied, can reveal to us 'la psychologie d'une âme, souvent celle d'un siècle, et parfois celle d'une race'.

This example reveals Taine's fondness for generalization and wideranging explanation, and he always loved, he tells us, 'sinon la métaphysique proprement dite, du moins la philosophie, c'est-à-dire les vues sur l'ensemble et sur le fond des choses', and we must now note that beyond even his claims to establish a scientific literary study, psychology and history he aspired, throughout his career, to find a method for nothing less than a scientific metaphysics. The positivist approach, he believed, gives us certainty – a view which is itself indicative of his over-confidence – but it cannot at present yield completeness of knowledge, a synthetic explanation of the whole of life and the universe. He found such an all-inclusiveness in the philosophies of Spinoza and Hegel, who influenced him from an early stage, but without certainty. He asserted that his own method of 'abstraction' could fuse the merits of their idealism and of positivism and lead us to 'l'absolue, l'indubitable, l'éternelle, l'universelle vérité'. By a process of successively repeated abstractions and verifications we can move from the causes of particular phenomena to the causes of those causes and ultimately grasp the supreme causes of universal life: at the summit of the pyramid of knowledge, he claimed, 'nous découvrons l'unité de l'univers'; we achieve the goal of metaphysics – by a method Taine asserts is scientific at every stage.

Not surprisingly, perhaps, even positivists like Mill rejected these views and thought he was ignoring 'the inherent limitations of human experience'. Taine's method may be modelled on that of the sciences, but since a Hegelian meaning is given to such notions as 'fact', 'law' and 'cause', it is certainly not, as he alleged, the scientific method itself. But Taine's confidence faded only in his final years; earlier he foresaw no limits to the scope and reliability of his approach and declared:

Dans cet emploi de la science et dans cette conception des choses il y a un art, une morale, une politique, une religion nouvelles, et c'est notre affaire aujourd'hui de les chercher.

This famous assertion reveals that like Comte he trusted that science could surmount its own boundaries and confirms that the real conclusion of his thought was a scientism of an even more audacious kind.

A similar judgement may fairly be passed upon others in the same positivist tradition – the famous chemist Berthelot, claiming that 'le triomphe universel de la science arrivera à assurer aux hommes le maximum possible de bonheur et de moralité'; in literature Zola, in *Le Roman expérimental* and *Le Docteur Pascal*; in sociology Espinas, Izoulet and Durkheim; and, in particular, Renan (1823–92), whose book on *L'Avenir de la science* (published in 1890 but written within four years of his break with the Roman Church in 1845) is the most exalted expression in the whole century of optimistic confidence in science – by which he especially meant the history of the human spirit, the 'science' of *philologie*. He ardently believed that this could save men from the 'shipwreck of scepticism' on moral and metaphysical questions which positivism might seem to have produced, that science could replace religion as a guide for mankind, and we shall later note his own version of its teaching.

La science est donc une religion [he proclaims]; la science seule fera désormais les symboles; la science seule peut résoudre à l'homme les éternels problèmes dont sa nature exige impérieusement la solution.

These thinkers claimed too much for the scientific method, one may well think, as regards both the potential area of its application and the certainty of its conclusions. Reality was exclusively equated with what is scientifically knowable, and the provisional, working determinism of the sciences was replaced by a form of fatalist determinism. Their excesses would soon provoke, as we shall see, a critical reaction that grew in strength in the final years of the century. Meanwhile, we must turn to the debates around a second major area of concern: religion.

Religious Orthodoxy, Doubt and Aspiration

'La religion naît de toutes parts', observed Bonald in 1796, and Napoleon's Concordat with the Pope in 1802 seemed to seal the official restoration of Catholic Christianity after the suppressions of the Revolution. A retreat from Voltairian irreligion marked the opening decades of the century, and a variety of factors conspired to strengthen the Church's position: social conservatism allied with fear of a return to revolutionary anarchy, Romantic religious feeling, the natural self-interest of priest and aristocrat, and from 1815 the restoration of the Bourbon monarchy. On the intellectual plane too the Catholic 'Traditionalists' were active and influential. Already in 1802 Chateaubriand's *Le Génie du christianisme* was contending that the truth of the Christian faith is shown by its unique ability to satisfy our inmost needs, by its beneficent and stabilizing impact on society, and by the rich aesthetic heritage it has inspired. Even his short novel *René*, he claimed, proves 'la puissance d'une religion qui peut seule fermer des plaies que tous les baumes de la terre ne sauraient guérir'. Louis de Bonald (1754–1840) and Joseph de Maistre (1753–1821) took an even more firmly orthodox stance, the former in works like his *Théorie du pouvoir politique et religieux dans la société civile* (1796) and the latter, most readably, in *Les Soirées de Saint-Pétersbourg* (1821). Their position is in strong reaction against the *philosophes* and the scientific attitude and expresses in its most forceful and uncompromising form the outlook of the so-called ultras. Society can only find a stable foundation in the authority of the Roman Church to curb human sin and pride and in the authority of a strong monarchy, which they believed to be the divinely ordained form of government. Lamennais, in his earlier work, supported the same views. His *Essai sur l'indifférence en matière de religion* (1817–23) attacked the principle of free examination and linked social dissolution with sceptical 'indifference' to the revealed moral truths of the Church. Individual reason, inner experience and the senses are alike distorted by illusion and error, and we should thus subordinate our personal judgement to the 'general reason' of mankind as a whole as enshrined in the values of 'tradition'.

A very different approach to Catholic faith is found in Maine de Biran (1766–1824). He began as a sensationalist, an admirer of Condillac and a member of the *idéologue* group, but the deeply introspective meditations described in his *Journal intime* (published in 1927) finally led him to replace his earlier scepticism by religious conviction. Whereas empiricism has normally regarded sense-experience – observation of the external world – as the main criterion of knowledge, Biran argues that our inner experience and reflection upon it are even more rewarding. Our immediate awareness of the reality in ourselves of conscious effort shows us that the self is primarily will (even more so than it is reason) and that, despite some physical determinism, it is ultimately free. We do not always utilize this freedom, for we tend to passivity as well as to action – as his treatise on *L'Influence de l'habitude sur la faculté de penser* (1803) examines – but in our 'vie active', and beyond that in our 'vie divine', the essential self finds its true expression. In his own day Biran was an original but little-appreciated philosopher in the tradition of French introspective writing, but later spiritualist thinkers – notably Bergson – were to draw upon his insights, and he has perhaps never been more highly respected than at the present day.

Other Catholics in the earlier nineteenth century were more socially involved. This is true to some extent of 'liberal Catholics' like Lacordaire and Montalembert during the 1830s and 1840s. They adopted a more moderate, less reactionary approach than Bonald and Maistre, and their influential journal, *Le Correspondant*, contributed to an undoubted resurgence of belief, amongst the bourgeoisie and upper classes at least, during the Second Empire period. And yet other Catholics went still further and, like Buchez and Ballanche, for example, propounded varieties of Christian socialism – and so, most famously, did Lamennais.

Lamennais (1782–1854) had become a priest in his mid-thirties and in his earlier work, we have noted, was a leading advocate for a conservative monarchy and for an ultramontane belief in the supreme authority of the Pope. No change of allegiance in the whole century, therefore, is more dramatic and arresting than Lamennais's conversion to a doctrine of democratic Christian socialism and his defiance of the papal censure of his views in 1832. In 1834 he published his most celebrated work, *Paroles d'un croyant*, written in high-flown biblical verses, a moving apologia for a Christianity of charity and brotherhood which has even been described as 'a lyrical version of the Communist

Manifesto'. To a present-day reader its ideas may seem too imprecise, dithyrambic and utopian, even though so deeply humane.

> Dans la cité de Dieu, tous sont égaux, aucun ne domine, car la justice seule y règne avec l'amour . . .
> Dans la cité de Dieu, nul ne sacrifie les autres à soi, mais chacun est prêt à se sacrifier pour les autres . . .
> Quand vous aurez rebâti la cité de Dieu, la terre refleurira, et les peuples refleuriront, parce que vous aurez vaincu les fils de Satan qui oppriment les peuples et désolent la terre, les hommes d'orgueil, les hommes de rapine, les hommes de meurtre et les hommes de peur.

Yet such poetic apostrophes, in chapter after chapter, spoke to the hearts of numerous radicals who, like him, were greatly disturbed by the poverty and inequalities of the newly industrialized conurbations. And the Pope's renewed condemnation of his views, which led him to break with the Church, seemed to his many admirers – including George Sand, Sainte-Beuve and other Romantics – to confirm that the Church was incompatible with the modern age. For them Lamennais and his book were important above all for what they symbolized – the idealistic integrity of the social prophet rejected by a reactionary priesthood. For the rest of his life Lamennais sided with the republican socialists of his day in such works as *Le Livre du peuple* (1837) and *De l'esclavage moderne* (1840). He retained a religious belief, expressed in his *Esquisse d'une philosophie* (1841–6), but died, somewhat embittered, without being reconciled with Rome. And indeed it is the case that the Church's general response, until almost the end of the century, to the scientific, intellectual, democratic and industrial challenges it encountered took the form of an ever firmer assertion of its authority – culminating in the *Syllabus of Errors* of 1864 and the proclamation in 1870 of papal infallibility in matters of faith and morals. And hence, whereas in England and Germany one finds many religious doubters who sought to adapt and to compromise with Protestant Christianity, in France most freethinkers felt compelled to oppose and to replace Catholic Christianity.

The state of the Roman Church at this time was, however, very far from being the sole factor which separated men from the Christian doctrines, and we must now survey the reasons underlying one of the most significant developments in nineteenth-century thought in France as elsewhere – namely, the widespread loss of belief in Christianity.

Unbelief in the late-seventeenth and eighteenth centuries had in general been aggressive and primarily rationalistic, confident that all religion is superstitious and reactionary. For the nineteenth century unbelief was far more often reluctant and even anguished – since both society and individual man were now felt to have need of religious faith – and was also and above all based on empirical and scientific grounds rather than on the sometimes callow rationalism of earlier sceptics. The rationalist contentions of the *philosophes* were certainly reiterated, however, and indeed strengthened by a still more confident appeal to the authority of science and the positivist philosophy: the so-called metaphysical proofs of God's existence are unsound; there is no place for supernatural intervention in a world ruled by natural laws; true knowledge derives from observation, whereas religion makes assertions about a realm that is in principle 'unknowable'. As to the alleged miracles of the Christian Gospels, they can be explained in naturalistic terms – as illusions, deceits or myths – an approach notoriously illustrated first in D. F. Strauss's *Life of Jesus* (1835, translated into French by Littré) and, no less controversially a little later, in Renan's *Vie de Jésus* (1863).

But in addition to these arguments nineteenth-century unbelievers were affected by much of the new scientific and historical knowledge of the day. It led them, first, to reject the doctrine of the literal infallibility of the Bible, at that time accepted by Catholics and Protestants alike. Geology reveals the world to be far older than the Bible narrative suggests. Zoology and biology, and especially the work of Lamarck and, later, Darwin, show man to have evolved from the animals, and if so the Creation story of the Book of Genesis must be historically false – not to add that it becomes harder to attribute to man a special, God-designed role in the world. Again, biblical scholars, applying the ordinary criteria of philological study, allege that there are inaccuracies and contradictions in the Scriptures and they are even led to question the doctrine of Christ's 'inerrancy'. Other historians contend that there is inadequate independent evidence to confirm the Gospel stories – nor, some add, is there any sign of God's providence at work in human history. Yet again, comparative philologists note the frequency in other ancient religions of allegedly miraculous events similar to those in the Bible and ask whether all the stories of virgin births, resurrections and ascensions may not stem from a common myth-making tendency in primitive man. Considerations such as these seemed decisive even to some practising Christians. The young Ernest Renan, for example, in training for holy orders at Saint-Sulpice, abandoned his faith in 1845 after a mere two years of philological study. His *Souvenirs d'enfance et de jeunesse* vividly describe the crisis he underwent and his central difficulty: if the Bible is proved to be fallible but the Roman Church proclaims it to be infallible, then the Church itself is in error and its claims to total authority are destroyed.

Physiological and psychological studies prompted another line of questioning: mind and body are so intimately linked that it is difficult to believe man has a soul (which has, in any case, never been observed) or that the soul could survive bodily death. And, more generally, both the Lamarckian and the Darwinian theories of evolution seemed able to give an account of the world and life in wholly naturalistic terms: thus, for example, the many signs of human and animal adaptation to environment do not oblige us to postulate a Divine Designer but can be explained as the outcome of an age-long, ruthless process of the survival of the best adapted. Well might Sainte-Beuve's Amaury, in *Volupté*, sum up the Lamarckian view in the words:

> La nature, à ses yeux, c'était la pierre et la cendre, le granit de la tombe, la mort! La vie n'y intervenait que comme un accident étrange . . .

These arguments that Christianity is unscientific and is contradicted by modern knowledge affected many anxious intellectuals, but no less widespread in their effects were various ethical contentions. First, it was alleged, certain Christian doctrines are immoral – notably the idea of eternal punishment in Hell for the unredeemed and also the substitutionary view of the Atonement, which holds that Christ died to satisfy God's demand that human sin be paid for, even if by an innocent substitute. Both rested upon a retributive theory of punishment that was being increasingly questioned, and both thus presupposed a morally repugnant idea of God. Poets like Vigny (in 'Le Mont des Oliviers'), Musset (in 'L'Espoir en Dieu') and Leconte de Lisle (in 'La Vision de Snorr' and 'Le Nazaréen') were particularly repelled, and the problem was made the more acute by the assertions of psychologists and sociologists that man's actions are determined by forces outside his control such as heredity and environment. And some even added that the Church's very doctrine of the Fall of Man diminishes the individual's responsibility for his sin – for which, all the same, it teaches that he may be eternally damned. Secondly, it was argued, the world itself is far from evidencing the alleged goodness of its

Creator; the cruelty and impassivity of nature, the ruthless struggle for survival highlighted by Lamarck and Darwin, the sufferings of disease and death, these seem rather to suggest a God who cannot be both morally perfect and omnipotent. And thirdly, it was contended, the moral and political attitudes of the Churches are often as immoral as their doctrines, marked by intolerant absolutism, worldly corruption and social apathy.

Forceful Christian replies to all these objections have not been lacking, and especially in the twentieth century, and it could well be argued that in response to them Christian teaching has now achieved greater clarity and hence force, has been purified of inessential accretions. In nineteenth-century France, however, the situation was still one of increasing conflict and polarization of beliefs, marked by ever more intransigent opposition between the adherents of Catholicism and *la libre pensée*.

Yet the unbelievers were in general far from being irreligious materialists. Regret for lost faith and the barrenness of religious scepticism became virtual commonplaces of French thought and literature at this time. 'J'étais incrédule, mais je détestais l'incredulité', wrote one Eclectic philosopher, and this reaction is typical of a time which Gérard de Nerval once called 'un siècle sceptique plutôt qu'incrédule'. Religion was prized as a basis for political stability, we saw, as a barrier against moral indifference, as an essential means to spur the masses to ethical action – and as much so by anti-Christian reformers like Comte and many of the socialistic reformers as by the Traditionalists. Furthermore, many of them recognized man's personal need for belief and expressed repeatedly their respect for his 'religious sentiment' – 'universal', 'indestructible', 'a fundamental law of his nature', as Constant's great work *De la religion* (1824–31) declared – for his sense of awed reverence as he surveys 'the starry heavens without and the moral law within'. Thus, for example, Michelet, following Constant and numerous other disciples of Kant and of Rousseau's Vicaire Savoyard, could say that religion is born 'presque toujours d'un vrai besoin du cœur', and a scientist like Claude Bernard declared: 'Il ne faut . . . pas chercher à éteindre la métaphysique ou le sentiment religieux de l'homme, mais l'éclairer et le faire monter plus haut'. And Renan could maintain – *after* his loss of Catholic faith: 'Ce qui est de l'humanité, ce qui par conséquent sera éternel comme elle, c'est le besoin religieux, la faculté religieuse.' These and many others could agree with Musset when he attacked Voltairian scepticism and spoke with dismay of 'le lait stérile de l'impiété'.

Consequently, whether for social or for personal reasons, the conviction spread that either the old religion must be restored or a new synthesis must replace it. Ballanche was typical when he reported in the early years of the century: 'Une nouvelle ère se prépare; le monde est en travail, les esprits sont attentifs.' These expectations were not to be disappointed, and it must be emphasized that the nineteenth century was not only critical in its intellectual life – critical of Christianity, critical of paternalistic government and *laissez-faire* economics – but was also a period of remarkable constructive enterprise and not only in the scientific realm. For all its scepticism this was an age that longed for infallibility – and found it, whether in the papal infallibility proclaimed first by the Traditionalists and later by the Church, or in the infallibility of science announced, as we saw, by Comte and other *scientistes*, or in the metaphysical infallibility claimed for Hegelian absolutism, or in the infallibility of progress as expounded by Marx and many other believers in a theoretical philosophy of history. Again and again any mood of scientific caution gave way to messianic hope and prophetic fervour, to the creation of new systems – new religions, indeed – to replace the discarded creeds of the past. It is arresting to note that this 'age of science' was also a time which rediscovered the fascination of magic and *spiritisme* (for Hugo was not the only one by a long way to be obsessed by 'les tables tournantes') and of occultism and illuminism – so influential as to leave their mark on literature from the Romantics and Baudelaire to Rimbaud, Huysmans and Villiers de l'Isle-Adam. Freemasonry became increasingly popular, and so did numerous minor religious sects, ranging from the Swedenborgians to such 'rational religions' as Victor Charbonnel's humanitarian cult in the 1850s, complete with its 'Human Christmas' and 'Festivals of Reason'.

New Creeds for Old

Of the many non-Christian creeds devised in the middle years of the century some merely borrowed the terminology of religion to lend an aroma of the infinite to purely ethical doctrines. Thus Vigny, writing at the conclusion of his *Servitude et grandeur militaires* (1835) about 'le naufrage universel des croyances', finds only one faith still intact – 'une dernière lampe dans un temple dévasté' – and without any sign of linguistic strain he goes on to describe his own stoic ethic as 'la religion de l'honneur' – 'une Religion mâle, sans symbole et sans images, sans dogme et sans cérémonies' – without the alleged accretions, that is, which alienated him from Christianity! And likewise Michelet, in *Le Peuple* (1846), described his ethic of French patriotism as a religion of fraternity: we should embrace 'la France, comme foi et comme religion'.

But many other thinkers went further and offered for men's worship a new deity, with new forms of religious service and new doctrines, even of immortality. Some proposed a primarily social religion, concerned to inspire man in his role as citizen: the 'new Christianity' of Saint-Simon and his disciples, Comte's 'religion of humanity', the creeds of Pierre Leroux (so enthusiastically admired by George Sand), Fourier, Cabet and his 'Icarians'. Others suggested primarily metaphysical religions which deified an explicitly metaphysical concept, such as Cousin's 'natural religion', based on reverence for 'the true, the beautiful and the good', and the religions of the 'Ideal' embraced by Renan and Vacherot. Yet others turned back to the non-Christian world-religions and mythologies popularized, we saw, by contemporary *philologues* and also by the many epic poems – from Hugo, Quinet, Ménard, Laprade and others – which reviewed the range of past religions in search amongst 'cette poussière divine' (in Quinet's words) for 'quelque débris de vérité, de révélation universelle'. Of these 'neo-pagan' creeds, as we may term them, some admired a single doctrine, and in particular Buddhism – as witness Senancour, Lamartine at certain moments, Vigny towards the end of his life, Leconte de Lisle, Brunetière, Amiel and others – whilst some hoped for a more comprehensive and eclectic faith, for some form of religious syncretism – as did Ménard and Ravaisson, Musset and Gérard de Nerval.

Even so brief an outline may suggest something of the profusion and diversity of these systems, but the great majority of them divinized either humanity or nature. In the former category, one of the most characteristic religious substitutes and the most successful in terms of durability proved to be Comte's positivist religion, to which he devoted much of his later career and which found adherents in England, North America, Brazil, Sweden and elsewhere as well as France.

Comte's first aim was to replace the unobservable deity of supernatural religion by a god that verifiably exists: he therefore proposed the new deity of 'Humanity', renamed 'le Grand Être', and if anyone protests that humanity is merely an abstract noun, his claim, like

Saint-Simon before him and Marx after him, was that on the contrary individual men exist only in and through mankind, the one true human reality. Secondly, he wished to avoid what he thought of as the other-worldliness and mysticism of supernatural faiths and to harmonize the everyday and religious lives. He believed this new worship would achieve this end, since the very preservation and development of the new deity become dependent upon our loving service. In future, he affirms, science, poetry and morality will be consecrated to the study, praise and love of humanity and our life will thus become a continuous act of worship. Comte acknowledges that men are at present self-centred, but he claims that his religious ethic based on love of mankind will cure this – especially with the help of a didactic art and literature, the beneficent moral influence of women, a political reorganization in which duties will take the place of rights, and above all the impact of a newly organized Church of Humanity. There is to be a hierarchy of priests – under Comte as high priest – and, like the Roman Church, holy festivals will be held – to celebrate now the basic social relations (marital, paternal, filial, and so on), now the earlier stages of man's religious development such as fetishism, and now various social groups – like womanhood (for which Comte had a particular veneration following his love for Clotilde de Vaux), the priesthood, the proletariat and even the capitalists. Again, there will be 'social sacraments' – beginning with 'presentation' (the equivalent of baptism) and ending with 'transformation' (burial) and, seven years after death, 'incorporation' into the great family of past humanity. So thorough was Comte that he even replaced the Christian calendar with months and saints' days named after great men like Aristotle and Archimedes and starting from 1789. As to immortality, he rejected the occultist notions which appealed to many of the utopian socialists of his day – ideas of metempsychosis, interstellar migration and the like; we live on after our death only by virtue of our thoughts and actions and their influence upon those who succeed us, but he believes that this 'subjective' existence is a 'noble immortality' and that extra moral impetus will stem from our desire to be counted and, in special festivals, commemorated as 'true servants of humanity', what his English followers somewhat humourlessly called 'the *holy* dead'.

This creed embodies a common and far from ignoble ambition in nineteenth-century secular thought: to satisfy religious aspiration by redirecting men's hopes and devotion towards the creation of a happier and more moral society on earth, and to do this by stressing practical

service in this world instead of a more mystical worship of a transcendental Being. Yet one may fairly wonder whether this faith can
inspire what for many people is the essence of religion – the sense of
the holy, awe before the infinitely perfect – and also note that Comte's
confidence in the potential goodness of man seems to be belied by the
authoritarianism of his religious and political proposals. And some
admirers of his earlier thought rejected these ideas: Littré suspected
he was insane and Mill was tempted to 'weep at this melancholy
decadence of a great intellect'. But others, no less idealistic, preserved
the 'Église Positiviste' into our own century, and, for example, the
last English 'Church', in Liverpool, only closed in the 1940s.

Probably the most popular substitute deity of the century was not
humanity, however, but nature, and in one guise or another many of
these new creeds were variants of the age-old doctrine of pantheism –
of the belief, essentially, that God is everything and everything is God.
Several different tendencies in the century's thought led to pantheism.
Even in Christian circles a marked emphasis was laid upon God's
immanence, His presence active in this world. But the Christians also
held fast to the counterbalancing doctrine of God's transcendence, His
existence in a transcendental realm: not so many unbelievers who
doubted precisely the reality of such a realm. Hence in Christian circles,
as the century advanced, there was a mounting – and fully warranted –
concern about the spread of pantheism. Romanticism, German idealism
(diffused in France by the Eclectics and others), occultism, the 'neo-
pagan' creeds already mentioned – all of these, or rather certain elements within them, converged on the same position. This is apparent,
first, in certain of the French Romantics, with their belief in the goodness of nature and their concept of 'Dieu en nous'. 'O nature! ô mère
éternelle!' declaimed Gérard de Nerval, linking nature-worship with
the cult of Isis. But in him and other poets like Lamartine and Hugo
we find only a vague, diffuse pantheism, not unlike that of Words-
worth. It became far more emphatic in philosophical circles under the
influence of Spinoza and especially Hegel. The world and in particular
human history are conceived to be a vast, implacably determined unity
moving towards the realization of an absolute of consciousness. Moreover, the criterion of historical necessity gives a criterion of moral
value: whatever is (in the long-term trends of history) is right. History
is seen as the working-out of a single design, as the product of a motive-
force that impels (it is often claimed) not only mankind but the whole
of nature. One good example amongst others is offered by the system

Renan devised after losing his Christian faith, his 'religion of the Ideal' as expressed in *L'Avenir de la science* and his *Dialogues philosophiques* (1876). He claims that a scientific study of universal history reveals a gradual but inevitable progression towards complete mental consciousness. This final goal he terms the Absolute, or the Ideal, or – just as readily – God. For the present 'God' exists in an 'ideal' state, but our moral duty is to work to bring 'God' into full reality, to fulfil the final end to which all history is moving. Such were the rudiments of the 'religion' which Renan then movingly embroidered with equivalents – non-supernatural equivalents – of the principal notions of Christianity: prayer as self-examination and meditation, a 'priesthood' of scholars, philosophers and poets, a form of immortality 'dans le souvenir de Dieu', and a future 'paradise' on earth. And this creed rested, as Renan himself made clear, upon a pantheistic belief that nature is good: 'Le mal, c'est de se révolter contre la nature ... Son but est bon; veuillons ce qu'elle veut.'

Other thinkers began not from Romantic sensibility or Germanic intellection but from science – from its postulation of the unity and determined interrelationship of the natural order. They then overlooked that this is merely a working hypothesis for the true scientist and claimed it to be a certainly known and supreme truth about the world. One need only add the further belief that nature is good, and one possesses the main elements of Saint-Simonian pantheism, which affirmed both the 'infinite unity' and the 'infinite, universal love' of the universe, and also of the ethic of stoical pantheism developed later by Taine. We saw that Taine's method for a 'scientific metaphysics' claims to lead us to the 'supreme cause' of nature: 'nous découvrons l'unité de l'univers et nous comprenons ce qui la produit'. And as we contemplate the beauties of nature, Taine affirmed, we feel that 'les choses sont divines' and experience 'la sublimité et l'éternité des choses'; this in turn inspires a serene confidence in the harmony of nature, fortitude in bearing our own sufferings, and a willingness to subordinate ourselves to the purposes of '[ce] Dieu universel dont je suis un des membres' – attitudes he believed were enshrined in the outlook of Marcus Aurelius and in the teaching of Hinduism and Greek polytheism. And, summing up his ethic, Taine arrestingly declares:

Il n'y a qu'un être parfait, la Nature; il n'y a qu'une idée parfaite, celle de la Nature; il n'y a qu'une vie parfaite, celle où la volonté de la Nature devient notre volonté.

One may feel that these pantheistic systems movingly revive man's age-old awe before the vastness and beauty of the universe. Yet it is also hard not to think that pantheism deifies merely what is biggest – 'le Grand Tout' so often hymned by these thinkers – and that scientific scrutiny may lead away from any belief in the universal moral goodness of nature or human history or individual human nature. We may sympathize with the dream, entertained by many ardent idealists like Cabet, Fourier and the Saint-Simonians, of a 'natural life', without vice or frustration, away from the corruptions of urban, capitalist society, a life in which virtue would become (in Taine's words) 'le fruit de l'instinct libre'. But the new model communities founded, in North America in particular, on the basis of this faith all too swiftly broke down, and if the Darwinian evidence of the cruelty of nature posed problems for the Christian, these were no less severe for the pantheist. Furthermore, as nineteenth-century critics like Renouvier stressed, pantheism rests upon a doctrine of universal determinism – a fatalism which tends to deny the reality of the individual.

More generally, it has to be conceded that little or nothing survived into the twentieth century of these religious substitutes – and of the others, syncretist, Buddhist and illuminist, that have been omitted here; even Comtism only remained alive in our own time with a much-diminished following. These creeds failed in part, one may suggest, because certain of them were authoritarian in an age of increasing liberalism: they offered (as T. H. Huxley said of Comte) 'Catholicism minus Christianity'; in part they failed because they lacked the efficient organization of an established Church and the inevitable vested interests which help to give it stability; in part because they lacked the emotional appeal of distant origins and an ancient tradition; in part because they tended to compete so publicly and stridently with each other. But above all perhaps they failed, for all their idealism, because what they were attempting was, if not impossible, harder than they appreciated. For many of these thinkers the very starting-point of their religious search was the assumption that there is no supernatural God, that any acceptable creed must be rational and scientifically based. But if religion is to be more than just (as Matthew Arnold held) 'morality touched with emotion', if its heart and its appeal to most men lie in a 'sense of the holy', of a 'mystery' beyond man's grasping, then we may wonder whether any effective religion can be confined within the rational and scientifically observable.

These difficulties may perhaps have weighed with other thinkers who were no less impelled to offer a new creed equal to the needs of the time – and who did indeed invoke sometimes the support of a new religion, like Cabet with his 'vrai christianisme' or Leroux with his 'religion métaphysique de l'humanité'. Yet in general, though tempted to imitate Saint-Simon's 'nouveau christianisme' or Lamennais's linking of Christianity and socialism, the many social reformers of the age – Charles Fourier, Étienne Cabet, Pierre Leroux, Proudhon, Louis Blanc and others – sought to give their ideas a quasi-religious appeal through a cult of history and progress.[1] Their individual systems naturally differed, but the cumulative impact of their writings – Fourier's *Le Nouveau Monde industriel* (1829–30), Cabet's romantic *Voyage en Icarie* (1842), Leroux's *De l'égalité* (1838) and *De l'humanité* (1840), Proudhon's celebrated *Qu'est-ce que la propriété?* (1840) (with its answer: 'La propriété, c'est le vol'), and Blanc's *L'Organisation du travail* (1839), amongst many others – was to provide a social and political rather than a religious solution for contemporary problems but to do so in messianic terms derived from an optimistic theory of historical inevitability. For most of them contended that history's age-long advance has brought us to the very threshold of a golden era in which will be vindicated the principle they themselves are advocating – social harmony for Fourier, fraternity for Blanc, equality for Leroux and also (though with a more ambivalent view of history) for Proudhon, liberty for yet others. By their critiques of industrial capitalism and their sometimes utopian plans for economic reorganization and social renewal – commonly through new model societies based on a communistic system of work and ownership – these thinkers have a major place in the early history of European socialism and helped to give it the optimism and prophetic idealism it still retains; the confidence they based on their faith in history would mark French socialism into our own age, as with socialists like Jean Jaurès and Léon Blum and Marxists like Jules Guesde.

Nor was the idealization of history and progress confined to social reformers; it is found in a very different form, usually with a Hegelian starting-point, in more metaphysical thinkers – notably Eclectics like

[1] On the social reformers and the historians of this period, cf. H. M. Peyre, in *French Literature from 1600 to the present* (London: Methuen, 1974), ch. 2. The fortunes of the ideas of progress and history are complex; for a fuller survey, cf. J. B. Bury, *The Idea of Progress*, 2nd ed. (New York: Dover, 1955), and D. G. Charlton, *Secular Religions in France (1815–1870)* (London: Oxford University Press, 1963), chs vii and viii.

Victor Cousin and Jouffroy and even certain Christian believers in divine providence. They were as convinced as the socialists that history is a unity, manifesting a single great design, motivated by a force transcending human control, moving beneficently towards (in the view of Cousin and his disciples) the realization of the absolute. The natural religion of the Eclectics was otherwise abstractly bare, based on worship of the metaphysical notions of the true, the beautiful and the good; it came nearest to gaining messianic appeal in its philosophy of history. (In Karl Marx, it may be added, one finds a fusion of the social and metaphysical theories, of socialism and Hegel, that helps to explain why his has proved the most formidable of all these deifications of historical inevitability.)

A host of other writers shared the mood of confident hope – whether derived from trust in scientific advance, from socialist progressivism, from Hegelian-type metaphysics, or from Christian belief in God. Hugo was characteristic when he declared in *Les Misérables*: 'L'éclosion future, l'éclosion prochaine du bien-être universel, est un phénomène divinement fatal . . . Le progrès marche; il fait le grand voyage humain et terrestre vers le céleste et le divin.'

Yet if a belief in progress encouraged many of the thinkers we have so far considered, it was to be increasingly challenged – already before the 1850s by such 'liberal' thinkers as Michelet and Quinet and historians like Guizot and De Tocqueville; later under the influence of political disillusionment following, first, the *coup d'état* of Louis-Napoléon and, in 1870-1, French defeat in the war with Prussia. One even finds growing evidence of what one scholar calls a 'sense of decadence' – after 1848 and still more after 1870.[1] And more generally too the intellectual tide was turning and slowly ebbing from the cults of science and history and the other 'secular religions' we have surveyed.

The Critical Reaction

In the first part of our period intellectual initiative has seemed to lie above all with thinkers who, having rejected Christianity, developed alternative philosophies based on science or progress, on socialism, a cult of humanity or a secularized pantheism, and marked by optimism about man and the power of human intelligence, by confidence in

[1] Cf. K. W. Swart, *The Sense of Decadence in Nineteenth-Century France* (The Hague: Nijhoff, 1964).

scientific method and informed social planning. This has rightly been described as 'l'époque des systèmes' – systems, in general, that purport to establish in one form or another a scientific humanism.

Gradually, however, from 1860 or 1870 onwards, the mood was modified. In some ways, certainly, the Third Republic was to be the very incarnation of reformist secularism and the universities seemed strongholds of anti-clerical and scientific thought, dominated by rationalists like Léon Brunschvicg (1869–1944) and such positivist sociologists as Émile Durkheim (1858–1917) and Lucien Lévy-Bruhl (1857–1939), who adopted a rigorously scientific approach both to sociology and to religion and ethics, which they considered to be useful products of social evolution now needing to be purged of their unscientific elements. Yet the final decades of the century appear in retrospect as a time of critical reaction against many of the ideas we have surveyed, as a time also when the outlooks of spiritualist philosophy and Catholic belief were reasserted more vigorously. This is not to imply that these outlooks had ever lacked strong advocates or that opposition to scientism had ever disappeared. On the contrary, scientists like Ampère (*Essai sur la philosophie des sciences*, 1834–43), Claude Bernard (*Introduction à l'étude de la médecine expérimentale*, 1865) and Théodule Ribot (*La Psychologie anglaise contemporaine*, 1870) all rejected the extravagant claims for science advanced by Saint-Simon, Comte and others and dissociated the true scientific attitude from belief in fatalism and materialism. Philosophers like Maine de Biran and the Eclectics led by Victor Cousin had argued during the earlier part of the century for a spiritualist and libertarian position. Philosophers of history like Quinet and Michelet had defended the reality and rights of individual liberty against authoritarian and determinist theories of inevitable progress. And in literature too concern for the 'ideal' was as strong in the Romantics as in Baudelaire and his fellow symbolists.

Yet only from the end of the Second Empire did the philosophical resistance to scientific humanism achieve a certain coherence and impact and the reaction against the positivists' dogmatic dismissal of the mysterious and spiritual in human life find wider diffusion in literature as well: in symbolist poetry; in the later plays of Dumas *fils* and the theatre of Maeterlinck, Villiers de l'Isle-Adam and others; in the Catholic literary revival of the late nineteenth century illustrated in Huysmans, Bloy, Jammes, Bourget and Claudel; in the naturalists' own rejection from around 1885 of Zola's preoccupation with material reality; in the literary criticism of Brunetière and others. Even the foreign authors who were most acclaimed in France at this time were interpreted as idealists who offered arms against the *scientistes* – Tennyson, Carlyle and Ruskin; Wagner, Schopenhauer and Hartmann amongst the Germans; Russian novelists like Tolstoy.

In philosophy this critical reaction was expressed above all in the work of the neo-criticist and idealist groups. The earliest of the neo-criticists was Cournot (1801–77), a difficult but penetrating thinker who was no less original in political economy than as an analytical philosopher. Philosophy for him was first and foremost a critique of the sciences; deeply influenced by Kant, like all the neo-criticists, his central concern was with the nature of knowledge, especially scientific knowledge. He claimed that Kant's notion of a scientific law was too rigid – for he had equated all science with mathematics and physics – and that the development of biology and sociology since Kant had shown that laws can attain no more than probability. To aspire to complete certainty, as Kant did in his *Critique of Pure Reason,* is to end with utter scepticism. Cournot, who began his career with work on mathematical theories of chance and probability, himself sought a middle way between Humean agnosticism and over-confident dogmatism; he conceived of a critique, he says, 'qui procéderait par voie d'induction probable, et non de démonstration positive'. Hence the essential problem of all knowledge, from the moment it passes from observations to generalizations and inductions, lies in the evaluation of probabilities. We must accept that 'l'absolu nous échappe', that we can never 'pénétrer l'essence des choses et en assigner les premiers principes'. But if we do acknowledge these limitations on our knowledge, then the way is open for us to affirm conclusions even in metaphysics, albeit they will never be more than tentative probabilities.

Contentions like these are plainly critical of the dogmatic assurance we have noted in the *scientistes*. They were to be reinforced, we shall see, by Lachelier and Boutroux and also by the works of Bernard and Ribot already mentioned, and similar views were to be authoritatively expressed a little later by the celebrated mathematician, Henri Poincaré, who in *La Science et l'hypothèse* (1902) and other books underlined that science, far from giving certain knowledge, can in principle offer no more than useful hypotheses of greater or lesser probability and subject to constant revision.

In addition to this epistemological argument the neo-criticists also stressed the problem of freedom and moral responsibility. Jules Lequier (1814–62), largely unknown in his day and influential only through his impact on Renouvier, has been hailed in our own time as a precursor of existentialism. His chief concern was with this problem, and his *Recherche d'une première vérité* (published by Renouvier in 1865) vividly describes his attempt to think his way through it without any appeal to his Catholic beliefs. He concludes that there is no compelling empirical evidence or rational argument that we are either free or determined; we are thus obliged to adopt a belief, to opt for or against free will, since knowledge is impossible. Determinism, he argues, destroys both moral responsibility and also the very possibility of an impartial search for truth (since, on that hypothesis, our statements are the products of extraneous factors), and he therefore urges, in a manner reminiscent of the argument of Pascal's 'wager', that we should choose to believe in the reality of our liberty. As he declares, in distinctly 'existentialist' terms,

Je préfère affirmer la liberté, et affirmer que je l'affirme au moyen de la liberté. Mon affirmation me sauve, m'affranchit. . . . C'est un acte de la liberté qui affirme la liberté.

Charles Renouvier (1815–1903), the leading neo-criticist and important both for his books and as editor of two important reviews, *La Critique philosophique* and *La Critique religieuse*, began from these notions of choice, belief and liberty but greatly widened their application. He agreed with the positivists that we only know phenomena but stressed against them that even this knowledge is incomplete and relative: we are never passive in the act of perception, our personality and especially our will are inevitably involved, and our knowledge thus always includes a 'personal' as well as an 'external' element. It follows for him that any certainty must be based on an act of will to believe, and he interprets the main problems of philosophy as a series of dilemmas on which a choice must be made. He himself opts for belief in free will, in an ethic which takes as its supreme value the fulfilment of individual personality, and in a pluralist notion of the world in which God exists but has only finite power, and he also emphasizes that if the individual is free, then progress is not inevitable and we are not subservient to historical necessity.

The neo-criticists may appear modest and unemphatic compared with the dogmatism they opposed, but to accept their arguments is to reject the claims to scientific certainty made by Comte, Taine and others as well as the assertions of metaphysical or theological certainty made by the Hegelians and the Roman Church, and it is also to dismiss materialism, fatalism, pantheism and the cult of history as mere metaphysical conjectures. These thinkers worked, in short, to undermine all the principal systems earlier in the century that we have surveyed, whilst at the same time, on the positive side, insisting on the free creativity of the individual and thus of society as a whole.

The idealist group of philosophers pursued similar lines of argument. Jules Lachelier (1832–1918) was particularly influential, partly through his teaching – his pupils included Bergson, Brunschvicg and Blondel, not to add Jaurès – and partly through his major book, *Du fondement de l'induction* (1871). Here he challenged the status of scientific laws by demanding how we can ever induce a law of allegedly infinite and permanent applicability from a finite number of previous observations. We can do so, he submits, only by virtue of two principles (the mechanist and the finalist) which our reason 'projects' on to the external world – principles, that is, which are not derived from sense-experience. It follows that we do not know the world as it is (as Comte and other 'realists' had asserted) but only as seen through the categories of our own mind.

Émile Boutroux (1845–1921) opposed scientism from a different standpoint. In his thesis, *De la contingence des lois de la nature* (1874), and later works he challenged the assumption – without which scientific laws cannot claim universal reliability – that a strict determinism rules in the natural order. Examining the actual workings of scientific study as well as its results, he contended that as we move from the physical to the biological sciences and on to the 'human sciences' we encounter an increasing area of 'contingency', of indeterminacy, and, at the human level, of liberty – a notion he sought to elaborate in his later ethical and religious thought.[1]

In retrospect the importance of these thinkers appears twofold. In the first place they initiated some of the principal tendencies of philosophy in the twentieth century – the movement towards a new spiritualism and a preoccupation with the themes of liberty, choice and personal creativity, for example. In the second place, by virtue of what they attacked they cleared the ground, as it were, for later French philosophy. By the mid-1880s the more confident forms of scientific humanism increasingly appeared as fallen idols. Some writers in their disillusionment relapsed into scepticism and pessimism or into a *fin de*

[1] Other idealist philosophers at this period are F. Ravaisson (1813–1900), É. Vacherot (1809–97) and A. Fouillée (1838–1912), in addition to late disciples of Eclecticism like Jules Simon and Paul Janet.

siècle cult of the self – like the young Anatole France, who had earlier revered Taine, or the Maurice Barrès of the trilogy of novels called *Le Culte du moi*, or Huysmans – earlier a disciple of Zola – at the stage he portrays under the guise of Des Esseintes in *A rebours*. Some returned to the Catholic Church, as did Huysmans and Barrès a little later, in common with Bourget, Claudel and others. Yet others moved from a philosophical to a political creed and, preserving something of their scientific humanism, embraced socialism in one guise or another – as, for example, did Anatole France. And still others were drawn by the ideas of new philosophers – and above all Henri Bergson, who both summed up in their most effective form the critical arguments just outlined and also presented the spiritualist philosophy in a way that was to appeal to some of the leading writers of the new generation – Péguy, Proust, Valéry, Gabriel Marcel and Louis Lavelle amongst others – and to prove a salient feature of the French intellectual scene in the twentieth century.

Henri Bergson

Henri Bergson (1859–1941) represented the culmination of the tradition of French spiritualism from Maine de Biran onwards and of opposition to nineteenth-century materialism and scientism, and at the same time he anticipated and indeed inspired some of the most significant developments in later French thought. He first won acclaim with his thesis in 1889, his *Essai sur les données immédiates de la conscience*, and after a period in schoolteaching, mainly in Paris, during which he published *Matière et mémoire* (1896), he became a lecturer at the École Normale in 1898 and, in 1900, professor of philosophy at the Collège de France. His other major works include *L'Évolution créatrice* (1907) and *Les Deux Sources de la morale et de la religion* (1932), and he also published an interesting study on *Le Rire* (1900) and a number of short but illuminating essays, of which *Introduction à la métaphysique* (1903) provides an especially useful summary of his philosophical attitude.

Bergson's achievement was both critical and constructive. The principal targets of his criticism were the positivist notion of determinism (in his *Essai*), materialism (in *Matière et mémoire*), mechanical concepts of evolution (in *L'Évolution créatrice*), and any primarily sociological interpretation of religion of the kind offered by Durkheim (in *Les Deux Sources*). And out of his attacks on these positions there emerged the positive themes of his own philosophy, as we shall see.

He contended that many nineteenth-century philosophers had equated science too narrowly with mathematics and physics – whence the deterministic, materialist and mechanistic notions he rejected. He himself, having acquired a detailed knowledge of biology, physiology and psychology, sought to derive from these more recent sciences a fresh approach to philosophy.

He began from the 'immediate data of consciousness' and observed a distinction he regarded as crucial between time as it is artificially measured for the ends of practical life and scientific experiment (by clocks, etc.) and time as 'la durée', time as I experience it – in which a few minutes of boredom may seem an hour or an hour of happiness may appear to pass in a few minutes. This in turn led him to distinguish between knowledge acquired by the intelligence – a faculty which has evolved for the purposes of action in the practical world, he believed – and inner experience or, as he termed it, 'intellectual intuition'. The intelligence is obliged, given its everyday goals, to split up the stream of time into separate 'moments', to divide an essentially continuous activity into separate stages. But this (as the paradoxes of Achilles and the tortoise and of Zeno's arrow illustrate) is to falsify the reality of things – a reality, he contended, that is ceaseless movement and change. The universe and everything in it is in a condition of unending 'flow', whereas the static 'snapshots' of life which we find useful in daily life or in scientific inquiries inevitably omit its essential elements of movement and duration. Only through the process of sympathetic self-immersion in duration which Bergson called 'intuition', 'a kind of intellectual sympathy', can we 'enter into' the reality of life. A symphony, for example, can be analysed intellectually into a succession of separate notes, but the essential nature of the symphony can be understood only if we experience it as a totality.

Two important examples of the intellect's distortion of reality are seen in the doctrines of determinism and materialism, Bergson believed. Our psychical life as we constantly know it contains an element of spontaneity, of freedom, manifested in action; it can only be reduced to a rigid causal chain of events if each event or act is taken in isolation – an approach which is falsifying. Taken as a whole the individual's mental life is free and creative. Similarly, he contends, our mental life cannot be reduced to purely material, cerebral events. He invokes physiological and psychological facts to show that the mind's activity conditions and overflows the activity of the brain: for instance, the psychopathological phenomenon of dual personality is independent of physiological change, he claims, and so also is our subconscious dream life. The brain is not consciousness itself but the organ of consciousness, through which consciousness enters into or affects matter. The phenomena of memories illustrate and confirm this analysis. Habit-memory – remembering how to walk or facts needed for daily life – is dependent on the brain, on 'physical traces' in the brain. But (as Proust's celebrated description of the working of 'involuntary memory' also reminds us) we possess as well a faculty of 'pure memory', through which we can gain a 'total recall' of past experiences that cannot be voluntarily remembered. Whereas the brain retains only the memories that are useful for life and dismisses, as it were, those other experiences which would otherwise overburden our consciousness, the mind retains all our past life (hence the feasibility of Proust's 'recherche du temps perdu') – and indeed gives us some assurance as to the permanence of the self, a self which is in other ways constantly changing.

Bergson also drew on biological science when he sought to provide an explanation of the facts of evolution. He criticized the two dominant theories provided by Lamarck and Darwin, both of which postulated a mechanical process without the intervention of mind or conscious purposes. He lists occurrences in the animal, vegetable and insect world which he claims cannot be accounted for in this way, and he also asks why, if the determining factor in evolution is no more than adaptation to environment, evolution did not cease many millennia ago. A very simple organism like the amoeba is very well adapted to survival; why, on this criterion, has life developed ever more complicated and hence endangered organisms? Bergson asserts that in reality there is an impulse driving life to take ever greater risks towards the goal of an ever higher efficiency, and this impulse he names 'l'élan vital' – a vital, creative surge, a psychological factor which pervades and drives on whatever is alive. This is the great force behind evolution. The factors isolated by the mechanists, such as the notion of adaptation, can explain the inner windings of evolutionary progress but cannot account for the general direction of its movement, still less the movement itself. And Bergson adds that the stream of change, of 'becoming', which is everywhere evident in organic life, is nothing other than this movement, this 'évolution créatrice', animated by 'l'élan vital', striving upwards, contending against the resistance of merely inert matter (whose existence, one may think, Bergson did not wholly explain), of the purely mechanical. (His criticism of mechanism is also reflected, one may add, in Le Rire, where he interprets laughter as a means – produced by evolution – whereby society seeks to discourage mechanical, inadaptable and thus ultimately antisocial behaviour by mocking those who are guilty of it.)

In his later career Bergson turned to a more serious consideration of religion and morality. He had earlier argued that metaphysical speculation by the traditional intellectual means must be misleading (since intellect has evolved for the ends of utility) and that some of the traditional metaphysical problems are in fact false dilemmas (like the so-called problem of free-will, as we noted). In *Les Deux Sources de la morale et de la religion* he advanced a more positive view that expanded the doctrines already seen of 'intellectual intuition' and of the individual's free creativity. He attacks the attempt, by Durkheim and others, to explain all religion and morality as the expression of social constraints or of psychological conditioning. Such 'static religion' and 'closed morality' do indeed exist, but Bergson urges us to study the religious and moral in their highest forms – as shown by such mystics as St John of the Cross, St Francis of Assisi and St Joan of Arc. In them we see religion linked with authentic spiritual experience, with an admirable balance of personality and with outflowing, creative love in action: they exemplify at their best 'la religion dynamique' and 'la morale ouverte'. Where 'closed morality' is the conventional ethic which society tries to impose on individuals to defend itself from chaos, 'open' or 'expanding' morality springs from the individual himself and his aspiration to a higher and more authentic level of moral goodness: it is essentially a personal invention.

Bergson's thought was expressed in a vivid, apparently lucid and even poetical style: it has even been suggested that this may have won some readers' assent to 'propositions which would hardly carry conviction if expressed in plain and sober prose'! Some critics have argued in particular that the insights of intuition are unverifiable and that Bergsonism thus condones irrationalism and subjective assertion, and they have also queried his account of material objects and his postulation of 'l'élan vital'. But however that may be, the effect of his ideas was refreshing and liberating, and by his positive assertions he also undoubtedly heralded some of the principal themes of existentialist philosophy. Both turn away from abstract intellection and closed dogmatics; both give primary emphasis to man's freedom and creativity and erect a vitalist form of humanism; both interpret moral values far less as standards outside ourselves, passively accepted by us, than as our own freely adopted inventions. Before turning to existentialism, however, we must now consider a second major manifestation of the spiritualist reaction in the twentieth century against the positivistic ideas of the nineteenth – namely, the renewal of Catholic thought.

The Catholic Revival

It is not surprising if to many observers around 1875 the Roman Church seemed to be in decline – assaulted by the arguments surveyed earlier in this chapter, dismissed by scientific humanists as irrelevant to the modern age, shorn of its territorial possessions and political power. The *Syllabus* of 1864, condemning such modern 'errors' as democracy, and the proclamation of papal infallibility at the Vatican Council of 1870 appeared to be rather desperate last-ditch attempts to reinforce a waning authority. But the outcome has been quite different – to the point that the renaissance of Catholic thought has proved one of the dominant features of the French intellectual scene in the twentieth century, matched only by the impact of Marxism, of Bergsonian philosophy, and of existentialism.

The Catholic revival was most evident in the later nineteenth century amongst literary writers – Barbey D'Aurevilly, Francis Jammes, and – more dramatically – other authors who were converted, within only a few years, from scientific naturalism or a sceptical cult of the self to Christian conviction. A novelist like Huysmans, earlier a naturalist admirer of Zola, evokes in *A rebours* (1884) the emptiness of an Epicurean search for novel sensations and in *En route* (1895) the motives which thereafter led him back to the Church, and in his later works he elaborates on the primarily personal and aesthetic reasons underlying his conversion. Bourget and Brunetière – having earlier been disciples of Taine – moved in the same direction, albeit more slowly and hesitantly, for primarily social and pragmatic motives: they prized Christian faith above all as a bulwark of moral and political order. Further illustrations are provided by Verlaine, by the young Paul Claudel, converted by a sudden experience in Notre-Dame-de-Paris in 1886, by Léon Bloy, Maurice Barrès and Charles Péguy, writers who created a tradition of Catholic literature that has been continued in more recent years by François Mauriac, Georges Bernanos, Gabriel Marcel and others.

In the realm of philosophy and theology this revival has been no less significant. The first and most orthodox group of French Catholic intellectuals who call for note are the Thomists – adherents of the thought of St Thomas Aquinas (1227-74), which had been proclaimed in 1879 as the official philosophy of the Roman Church, and closely linked with an international group of theological scholars (notably, Cardinal Mercier in Belgium). Jacques Maritain began as a Protestant admirer of Bergson, but after his conversion to Rome became a major Catholic thinker, influential both by his restatement of scholastic ideas in such works as *Saint Thomas d'Aquin apôtre des temps modernes* (1923) and *Primauté du spirituel* (1927) and by his attacks on post-medieval individualism and irrationalism. Amongst contemporary thinkers he particularly attacked Bergson – notably in *La Philosophie bergsonienne* (1914), the more striking since written by an erstwhile disciple. He can praise Bergson for his attacks on materialism, scientism and Kantian relativism but condemns him for his anti-intellectualist standpoint. Bergson's denial that our intellect can know reality opens the way to a new phenomenalism, a subjectivism that is inevitably in conflict with Thomist 'realism'. Similarly and more widely, Maritain contends, the Renaissance, the Reformation and Cartesianism represented in their break with scholastic orthodoxy an assertion of individualistic pride and error – a judgement expanded in *Antimoderne* (1922) and in his studies of Luther, Descartes and Rousseau in *Trois Réformateurs* (1925). Étienne Gilson has been equally forceful in expounding medieval philosophy – in studies like *La Philosophie au moyen âge* (1922; revised ed. 1944) and *L'Esprit de la philosophie médiévale* (1931-2) and also through his teaching at the Collège de France and the University of Toronto – and the reaffirmation of the scholastic outlook has been strengthened also by reviews like the *Annales de philosophie chrétienne*, the *Revue néo-scolastique* and the *Revue thomiste*. The achievement of these thinkers has been above all to re-examine and restate the Thomist teaching, to extend it by reference to modern knowledge, and to argue its relevance to the present age – a tendency seen also in the Dominican scholar A. D. Sertillanges. His expository works on *Saint Thomas d'Aquin* (1910) and *Les Grandes Thèses de la philosophie thomiste* (1928) stressed the need to 'nourrir par le dedans ce vivant qu'est le système en lui faisant assimiler toute la substance nutritive que les siècles ont depuis élaborée', and in his work on *Le Christianisme et les philosophies* (1941) he described 'le travail de rénovation' Thomism must undergo, in his view, in order to be fully revivified.

The Thomists represent the most traditionalist aspect of the Catholic renaissance. Other thinkers have moved in more 'modernist' directions; they offer new variations on the permanent themes of Catholic doctrine. They have sought to reinterpret the old faith in the light of modern ideas, whether Bergsonism (as with Édouard Le Roy) or existentialism (as with Gabriel Marcel). This is not to imply that most of them strayed into the full modernist 'heresy' which was condemned by Rome in 1907. Alfred Loisy (1857–1940) was almost alone in doing so (though Loyson went still further). Loisy was on the staff of the Institut Catholique in Paris, until he was dismissed in 1894 on account of his unorthodox ideas, and later became professor of the history of religions, from 1909 to 1932, at the Collège de France. His views are well indicated by his controversial book on *L'Évangile et l'église* (1902). His work on biblical criticism led him, first, to follow in the steps of Renan by denying the Church's doctrine on biblical infallibility: the Pentateuch (for instance) cannot be considered the work of Moses but is the product of successive generations, and the Gospels were probably compiled in a similar manner. He also interpreted Christ's teaching in primarily moral terms and denied that the Church was explicitly established by Christ or had any consequent right to impose its dogmas on the individual Christian.

Less unorthodox and in the long term more influential was the development of a Catholic 'philosophy of action'. This found its basis in the thought of Léon Ollé-Laprune (1830–99) and was developed more fully by Maurice Blondel (1861–1949) and the Abbé Laberthonnière (1860–1932). Ollé-Laprune rejected a merely abstract or intellectual concept of knowledge so far as moral truths are concerned. He stressed the primacy of practical reason, the role and dynamism of the will and the importance of creative action. 'Les vérités morales, règle pour la volonté en même temps que lumière pour l'esprit [he declares in his first major book, *De la certitude morale* (1880)], exigent un acte moral, un acte conforme à leur nature même, pour être pleinement reconnues et acceptées.' This approach was adopted by Blondel – as is indicated by the title of his doctoral thesis and best-known work, *L'Action: Essai d'une critique de la vie et d'une science de la pratique* (1893). Our life is above all a life of action, and philosophy should thus deal with this rather than with merely theoretical speculations. Action transcends the grasp of intellect (a view parallel to Bergson's) and is above all an expression of the will. In words that clearly anticipate the existentialist attitude Blondel proclaims: 'Nous sommes engagés et nous agissons, nous optons, que nous le voulions ou que nous ne le voulions pas. Ne pas faire, c'est encore se décider. Un enfant se noie; ne pas se décider à aller porter secours, c'est se décider contre.' Hence his opposition to dilettantism of the kind adopted by the young Maurice Barrès, for this fails to take seriously the consequences of our acts, and also to pessimism which preaches their ultimate pointlessness. On the contrary, Blondel believes, since action strives to attain some end beyond itself it presupposes a reality superior to action – a reality he claims to be divine and both immanent in man and also transcendent. For him, therefore, our actions are 'sacramental' – the manifestation of the divine that is both within us and beyond us – and to examine the life of action is to be led to a religious faith in God and in love as the ultimate good.

Another illustration of a Catholic modernism that opposes Thomism is offered by Édouard Le Roy (1870–1954), who was deeply influenced by Bergson. His primary aim was to reconcile Christian faith with science and philosophy. He continued his master's attack on the dogmas of scientism by maintaining that scientific laws, far from corresponding with reality, are artificial, even arbitrary, although useful constructs. The regularity and determinism which Taine and others attributed to the natural order are in fact the creation of the scientists themselves. But Le Roy also attacked the dogmatism of theology and particularly of the Thomists, notably in his *Dogme et critique* (1907) and *Le Problème de Dieu* (1929). Religious doctrines, like scientific laws, are useful and practical: they serve to exclude errors and guide us as to how we should act, but they cannot circumscribe ultimate truth or reduce it to a set of formulae. His more positive ideas, in such works as *Les Origines humaines et l'évolution de l'intelligence* (1930), developed the Bergsonian notion of creative evolution but have proved less durable, other than his stress on a practical and open moral idealism.

Other modernists active at this period included the Abbé Laberthonnière, who expanded Blondel's ideas, and Jacques Chevalier, who sought to link Bergson's thought with earlier philosophy, and one may sum up the main concerns of all these thinkers as being to fuse the old doctrines with new knowledge and preoccupations, to emphasize a vitalist and creative notion of man, and to oppose abstract philosophical and theological intellection. From the standpoint of the Roman Church certain of them fell into heresy: Loisy was excommunicated in 1908, and works by others were placed on the Index. None the less their thought has remained active and did in fact prefigure several contemporary trends within Catholicism – the 'personalism' of Emmanuel Mounier, the movement of 'la Philosophie de l'esprit' led by René Le Senne and Louis Lavelle, the ideas of Teilhard

de Chardin, and, even earlier, Gabriel Marcel's Christian version of
existentialism – the third dominant development in French thought in
our century which we must now outline.

Existentialism

Existentialism tends to be considered a distinctively contemporary
intellectual movement, stimulated by French experience under Nazi
occupation and expressed in the works of wartime and post-war
writers. Yet the first clearly existentialist thinker lived well over a
hundred years ago – Sören Kierkegaard (1813–55), a deeply anguished
Danish Christian – and in our own age German philosophy was much
affected by such thinkers as Karl Jaspers and Martin Heidegger well
before the rise of Hitler. In France Gabriel Marcel (1889–1973) was
writing existentialist plays and essays from the 1920s onwards and
Louis Lavelle's first two books appeared in 1921. The authors we most
often connect with this movement – Sartre (b. 1905), Simone de
Beauvoir (b. 1908), Maurice Merleau-Ponty (1906–61) and, to some
degree, Camus and others – are in fact expanding and popularizing an
already well-founded philosophy. If their thought has had a wider
impact than their predecessors', this is because most of them have
succeeded in conveying its ideas in the vivid and concrete modes of
imaginative literature as well as in speculative writings. Comparatively
few readers have studied (say) Sartre's *L'Être et le néant* (1943), his
major and lengthy philosophical essay in 'phenomenological ontology',
but his plays and novels have directly expressed its main themes to
countless readers and spectators. Indeed, related to this fact, contemporary existentialism has almost certainly had less effect on professional
philosophy than it has exerted on a wider audience as a body of general
attitudes and ideas – and it is on this aspect that (for lack of space) we
shall concentrate here.

It is arresting – at first sight at least – to note that the existentialist
position has been expounded by both Christians such as Marcel and
atheists like Sartre. What are the ideas which all of them hold in common? In the first place, they are all in reaction against abstract, in-
tellectualist philosophy. Just as Kierkegaard began by opposing the
rationalist metaphysics of Hegel, so his modern successors contend that
most academic philosophers have been less concerned with the imperative problems posed by man's personal situation than with largely
unreal or trivial questions. They have also thought primarily in terms

of essences and universals – as when Plato describes the world as a mere reflection of the world of abstract ideas or Aristotle and many others seek to derive an ethic from a notion of 'universal human nature' to which each individual should seek to conform. The existentialists, on the contrary, assert the priority of existence over essence (an affirmation we shall return to) and press us to think in concrete terms about the actual problems of our existence. The 'essentialist' thinkers, moreover, emphasize rationality and objectivity as the prime desiderata of philosophy; the existentialists, on the other hand, are avowedly subjective. They are so, first, in that their concern is with the individual and his predicament – caught up in the dilemmas and sufferings of life and confronting his own inevitable death: hence in part their fondness for diary and meditation forms of writing – as illustrated by Antoine's diary in *La Nausée*, Rieux's diary in *La Peste*, or Marcel's *Journal métaphysique*, for instance. And they are so, secondly, in that their purpose is to appeal not only to their reader's intellect but to 'the whole man', man as subject: hence their belief that literary forms may offer more adequate means of communication than philosophical prose, that (in Simone de Beauvoir's characteristic words) 'seul le roman permettra d'évoquer dans sa réalité complète, singulière, temporelle, le jaillissement originel de l'existence'.

These attitudes stem from a preoccupation with existence, and these thinkers are all urging us to become more fully aware of the fact and implications of our existing. Many people pass their life in a dream, as it were, in a state of non-reflexion and habit, searching only for a passive state of satisfaction, without ever considering their true situation – the chanciness of the very existence of the world and themselves, the moral choices which life challenges them to make, the inevitability of their death. Pascal (often invoked as a precursor of existentialism) could declare: 'Je m'effraie et m'étonne de me voir ici plutôt que là, car il n'y a point de raison pourquoi ici plutôt que là, pourquoi à présent plutôt que lors.' So, likewise, the existentialists feel (in Marcel's words) that 'l'existence n'est pas séparable de l'étonnement'. Furthermore, we neglect all too often the existence of others as well as of ourselves – as when we treat them as mere objects which are useful or injurious to us – in the manner, at worst, of Nazism, but no less commonly in our daily lives where we only rarely achieve what Marcel terms 'true inter-subjectivity' and meet other people 'in openness'.

But existence is a highly ambiguous term. These writers distinguish three kinds of existence in particular – for which a German terminology developed by Heidegger and others is most helpful. 'Vorhandensein' indicates the existence of inanimate objects. 'Dasein' indicates the existence of animals – and of humans in so far as they exist for (say) government officials. 'Existenz', in contrast, may be translated as 'full existence' – 'really living' as opposed to 'merely existing'; it involves an active 'engagement' in life as opposed to the passive engagement of 'Dasein'. It fundamentally implies developing oneself and realizing one's potentialities; it presupposes constant change – and not the passive change undergone (say) by heated metal or freezing water, but an active, conscious, willed change that derives from choice and freedom. And since only man has freedom to choose in this way, it follows that 'Existenz' is the special, distinguishing prerogative of man.

Yet many people do not utilize their freedom; they accept society's conventional values and share its mass reactions. And hence the existentialists seek to insist that one must choose one's own values, utilize one's freedom in an authentic way, create one's own essential self – and here is another way in which existence precedes essence, for what I essentially have been will only be finally fixed when I no longer exist. They do of course accept that we are all determined to some extent by external factors – society, class, education, heredity, and so on – but they assert that we still retain freedom as to the ways in which we react to these conditioning factors.

To choose implies motives and standards for choice, however. Yet these are not evident, they believe, do not obviously inhere in the objective world. Even the Christian existentialists are conscious of a metaphysical darkness, an apparent irrationality, in the world. Pascal urged man in this situation to 'wager', and Kierkegaard postulated the need for a 'leap of faith'. The modern existentialists agree that each man must adopt his own values, but atheists and Christians differ as to the values they support, as we must now see – just as, indeed, their statements of even this common outlook naturally reveal somewhat differing emphases.

The first distinctive stress of atheists like Sartre is upon the experience of 'absurdity', of (in the title of Sartre's first novel) 'la nausée'. This sense of the meaninglessness of life and of revulsion from it and from other people seems to have four principal sources. First, since God does not exist in their view it follows that there is no objective, 'God-given', purpose in human life. Like Nietzsche and Malraux before them, Sartre and Camus (who shared some existentialist notions whilst rejecting others) realize the vast moral consequences of 'the death of God'. Whereas earlier atheist humanists asserted that accepted moral values remain no less imperative even without a deity to validate them, the existentialist, Sartre tells us, 'pense qu'il est très gênant que Dieu n'existe pas, car avec lui disparaît toute possibilité de trouver des valeurs dans un ciel intelligible'. The feeling of absurdity derives, secondly, from the inevitability of our death: given this final end (for it is assumed by these thinkers that we enter no after-life), no value or purpose can have any ultimate status for us. Thirdly, we observe that the world and all within it are contingent, fortuitous, finally inexplicable. Nothing is 'necessary', and at times, therefore, the existentialist feels disgust at the sight of objects (such as the chestnut tree described in *La Nausée*), of other people, and even of himself. And this feeling of the pointlessness, the superfluous quality of people is heightened as we observe them (and ourselves) leading a life of habit, of passive conventionality.

Yet fully to realize our absurd situation need not be depressing; on the contrary, we are liberated to live our own existence untrammelled by fear of divine punishment, moral conventions, or hope and concern for the future. At times, certainly, our total freedom will weigh upon us: we are (Sartre notes) 'condemned' to be free, and though each of us is 'un projet', 'une liberté pure', we have no obvious criteria to guide our choices. But even this can be reinvigorating and challenging – as Hugo in Sartre's *Les Mains sales* finds when he finally affirms his justification for killing Hoederer. Furthermore, these thinkers do suggest that there are at least some signposts as to how we should live – and here one may discern indications of the old humanist values they began by rejecting! Thus Sartre contends that, since all that is 'given' is man's liberty, we should embrace that liberty as a supreme value; we should be constrained in our choices by a sense of responsibility to others and by the imperative of freedom – for others as well as ourselves. He also urges that we should seek to live 'authentically', without falling into that deception of others and of ourselves which marks 'la mauvaise foi', and he adds that only by living in this wholly honest way can we establish fruitful and genuine relations with other people. At first sight others appear to menace and delimit our own freedom, and in the face of their challenge we may be tempted either to surrender to them – to conform to what they want us to be (the reaction Hugo finally rejects at the conclusion of *Les Mains sales*) – or to fight against them (the reaction of the characters in *Huis-clos*, a play ending with the words: 'L'enfer, c'est les autres.'). But either response brings frustration, deceit, hypocrisy, and makes men into enemies; by contrast, 'authenticity' allows us to achieve a new relation of equality and friendship with others.

Sartre has turned increasingly to the political arena since he first expounded these ideas, but the leading French representative of existentialist *Christianity*, Gabriel Marcel, remained concerned above all with the individual person and his relations with other individuals.

It may first be noted that Christianity is in several ways an existentialist religion *avant la lettre*. It has always stressed the existential reality of God Himself – a personal Being, not a mere First Cause or abstract principle, a God 'who was made flesh and dwelt amongst us', a God with whom men can achieve a personal link – and equally of each human individual, eternally himself. The Christian faith also emphasizes each person's moral freedom and responsibility and the imperative of choice. In addition, some Christians have experienced a deep sense of anguish before life's irrationality – a tradition illustrated, for example, by Tertullien, Augustine and Pascal, underlying also the theology of predestination, and most clearly related to existentialist themes by Kierkegaard.

Marcel is less anguished than they, however, and manifests greater confidence in divine justice than at least Kierkegaard. He was converted to Catholicism in 1929, but well before that he was keeping his *Journal métaphysique* (*1913–1923*) (published 1928) and writing his first plays. Yet his major philosophical essays come later – notably *Être et avoir* (1935), *Homo Viator* (1945) and *Le Mystère de l'être* (1949–50) – the last consisting of particularly probing lectures – and his mature thought is basically Christian as well as existentialist.

Marcel is deliberately unsystematic in his thinking: to summarize his outlook is to risk reducing it to a quite misleading orderliness. His aims are to stimulate awareness and contemplation about man's situation and, in a discursive manner, to explore certain experiences and aspects of life which seem to him significant. He does not wish to impose a philosophy upon his readers, to compel their assent, but rather to solicit them to find a philosophy of their own, to achieve a belief that must be personal and involve personal commitment. This attitude follows from certain of the principal themes of his own meditations. He is first and above all aware of the 'mystery of being' – the mysterious in life itself and the universe, in the religious order, and especially in the individual. The question: 'Who am I?' dominates an early play like *Un Homme de Dieu* (1925) and is reiterated throughout his work, both essays and plays, many of whose characters are seeking to 'know themselves'. To plumb this realm of the mysterious cannot be achieved by a reasoning that is abstract, mathematical, systematic, he contends; the kind of reason apt for this task must be concrete, intuitive, contemplative – what he terms 'la réflexion' – and hence he defines metaphysics as 'la réflexion braquée sur un mystère'. He also stresses that this contemplative process of inquiry should begin not from abstractions or *a priori* notions but from experience – from one's personal experience in particular, for Marcel is less interested in sensory observations than in man's inner, spiritual life. Thus he declares: 'L'expérience s'intimise pour ainsi dire et s'exerce à reconnaître ses implications.' Moreover, he points out, my basic experience of myself is less of an object than of a subject: whereas we observe an object from without, we identify ourselves with a subject, and Marcel argues that a particularly significant kind of knowledge comes from such 'participation', especially as found in our acquaintance with other people. Indeed, he claims that love is the only starting-point for a complete understanding of persons and the 'mysteries' of interpersonal existence.

The distinction of subject and object is linked for him with other, parallel distinctions. Thus he juxtaposes the realms of 'being' and of 'having': 'l'avoir est tout ce qui peut être aliéné; l'être, c'est l'inaliénable, l'intransmissible'. And whilst the world of 'having', of objects and of persons treated as objects, presents 'problems' which can be solved by reason and calculation, the world of 'being', of subjects, confronts us with 'mysteries' with which we are personally 'engaged' and which are not amenable to 'solutions'. Regrettably, the modern technological world treats people as mere 'fonctionnaires', that is as objects, reduces life to a series of 'problems' to be solved, evaluates it in terms of 'having', of profitability and possessions, and increasingly deprives men of their privacy – and thereby of the inwardness, imagination and creativity that go with it. We live in a 'broken world', Marcel asserts – of the kind portrayed in his play of 1933, *Le Monde cassé*: 'Chacun a son coin, sa petite affaire, ses petits intérêts. On se rencontre, on s'entrechoque . . . Mais il n'y a plus de centre, plus de vie, nulle part.'

The link between these themes and Christianity is evident, and in addition Marcel stresses our experience of a 'transcendental' dimension and interprets Christian belief as centred on belief in a person, Christ, and on achieving full 'intersubjectivity' between man and man and

God and man. In 1950 existentialism was the object of papal condemnation – for its irrationalism, individualism, subjectivism and pessimism,
amongst other reasons. But these charges would seem to leave almost
wholly unscathed Marcel's contemplative, human and – in his own
word – 'neo-Socratic' Catholicism.

More generally, however, Marcel illustrated one of the ways in
which even Catholic thought has moved, in some of its exponents, in
the same directions as have been discerned in Bergsonism and the
atheist existentialists. Amongst other Catholic examples we can only
note, for lack of space, the 'personalism' of Emmanuel Mounier (1905–
50), best expressed in the pages of his review *Esprit* and in such books as
Le Personnalisme (1949), and the movement of 'la Philosophie de
l'esprit' founded by René Le Senne and Louis Lavelle (1883–1951) and
most fully developed in Lavelle's philosophical works, notably *La
Dialectique de l'éternel présent* (4 vols, 1928–51). What are these common
tendencies – which can also be discerned in literary writers from Péguy
and Gide to Malraux and Saint-Exupéry? We may summarize them,
all too briefly, as a movement away from traditional philosophy and
towards a more undogmatic and personal commitment; towards a
primary emphasis on man's freedom and creativity and on a vitalist
humanism; towards a conception of moral values less as rules accepted
from outside ourselves than as our own personally adopted inventions.
Important differences naturally persist, but underlying them one finds
affinities both in what is rejected – the authoritarianism of those earlier
nineteenth-century attitudes which this chapter began by surveying in
positivists and Catholics alike – and in what these contemporary
thinkers aspire to achieve: a largely undogmatic adumbration of a
humane, creative personalism.

Bibliography

GENERAL

Less attention has been given to nineteenth- than to twentieth-century French
thought in recent decades, even in France itself, social and political ideas alone
excepted, and even major texts by nineteenth-century philosophers are not always
easy to find in print. Standard French histories of philosophy are É. Bréhier,
Histoire de la philosophie: La Philosophie moderne, Vols III and IV (Paris, 1932;
English translation, Chicago, 1968–9); J. Chevalier, *Histoire de la pensée*, Vol. IV:
La Pensée moderne (Paris, 1966); L. Lévy-Bruhl, *History of Modern Philosophy in
France* (London, 1899); V. Delbos, *La Philosophie française* (Paris, 1919); and, for

the period since *c*. 1870, I. Benrubi, *Les Sources et les courants de la philosophie contemporaine en France*, 2 vols (Paris, 1933); J. Guitton, *Regards sur la pensée française, 1870–1940* (Paris, 1968); L. Lavelle, *La Philosophie française entre les deux guerres* (Paris, 1942); and D. Parodi, *La Philosophie contemporaine en France* (Paris, 1919). Briefer studies in French, providing a more rapid survey, are A. Cresson, *Les Courants de la pensée philosophique française*, 2nd ed., Vol. II (Paris, 1931); J. Lacroix, *Marxisme, existentialisme, personnalisme* (Paris, 1951); and J. Wahl, *Tableau de la philosophie française* (Paris, 1962). In English, three lucid but now somewhat dated works are G. Boas, *French Philosophies of the Romantic Period*, 2nd ed. (New York, 1964); A. L. Guérard, *French Prophets of Yesterday* (London, 1913); and J. A. Gunn, *Modern French Philosophy (1851–1921)* (London, 1922). A more recent survey of nineteenth-century thought is given by D. G. Charlton, *Secular Religions in France (1815–1870)* (London, 1963), and on twentieth-century thinkers there are M. Farber (ed.), *Philosophic Thought in France and the United States* (New York, 1950), and C. Smith, *Contemporary French Philosophy* (London, 1964) – both of them offering useful studies in English.

CATHOLICS

A long-standing and still illuminating study of one strand in Catholic thought is G. Weill, *Histoire du catholicisme libéral en France (1828–1908)* (Paris, 1909), whilst wider and authoritative studies are A. Dansette, *Histoire religieuse de la France contemporaine*, 2 vols (Paris, 1951–2), and L. Foucher, *La Philosophie catholique en France au dix-neuvième siècle* (Paris, 1955). Briefer studies, which also discuss literary writers, are provided by J. Calvet, *Le Renouveau catholique dans la littérature contemporaine* (Paris, 1931); H. Guillemin, *Histoire des catholiques français (1815–1905)* (Paris, 1947); and V. Giraud, *De Chateaubriand à Brunetière: Essai sur le mouvement catholique en France au dix-neuvième siècle* (Paris, 1938). On one important development there is the major work of J. B. Duroselle, *Les Débuts du catholicisme social en France (1822–1870)* (Paris, 1951), and on modernism two books by E. Poulat, *Histoire, dogme et critique dans la crise moderniste* (Paris, 1962), and *Alfred Loisy: sa vie, son œuvre* (Paris, 1960). On the 'philosophy of action' there are H. Duméry, *La Philosophie de l'action* (Paris, 1948), and J. Paliard, *Maurice Blondel ou le dépassement chrétien* (Paris, 1950). A helpful study of its subject in English is B. Menczer, *Catholic Political Thought, 1789–1848* (London, 1952).

POSITIVISTS

In French there is a long-standing major study of one aspect of the positivist movement by S. Charléty, *Histoire du saint-simonisme*, 2nd ed. (Paris, 1931), but more of the general surveys, surprisingly, are in English: D. G. Charlton, *Positivist Thought in France (1852–1870)* (Oxford, 1959); F. A. Hayek, *The Counter-Revolution of Science* (Glencoe, Ill., 1942) (written, however, from a particular critical viewpoint); and chapters in F. E. Manuel, *The Prophets of Paris* (Cambridge, Mass., 1962). On individual thinkers most studies are naturally in French. On Comte, two difficult but major works are J. Delvolvé, *Réflexions sur la pensée comtienne* (Paris, 1932), and P. Ducassé, *Méthode et intuition chez A. Comte* (Paris, 1939), to which one may add an older but still valuable study in G. Dumas, *Psychologie de deux messies positivistes: Saint-Simon et A. Comte* (Paris, 1905), and an authoritative historical survey in H. Gouhier, *La Jeunesse d'A. Comte et la formation du positivisme*, 3 vols (Paris, 1933–41). Useful short expositions are G. Cantecor, *Comte* (Paris, n.d.); A. Cresson, *Comte* (Paris, 1941); and (from a somewhat uncritical admirer) P. Arnaud, *Pour connaître la pensée d'A. Comte* (Paris, 1969). Two most interesting and, at their time, influential analyses by philosophers who were themselves much affected by Comte's earlier thought (but rejected his later religious ideas) are É. Littré, *A. Comte et la philosophie positive*, 2nd ed. (Paris, 1864), and J. S. Mill, *A. Comte and Positivism*, 2nd ed. (London, 1866). On Taine, the major studies in French are still G. Barzellotti, *La Philosophie de Taine* (Paris, 1900), and A. Chevrillon, *Taine: Formation de sa pensée* (Paris, 1932); good shorter treatment is found in M. Leroy, *Taine* (Paris, 1933), and P. V. Rubov, *Taine: Étapes de son œuvre* (Paris, 1930). In English there is little – a chapter in Charlton, op. cit., and (on his thought as a would-be scientific cultural historian) S. J. Kahn, *Science and Aesthetic Judgment* (London, 1953). On Renan as a thinker the works of J. Pommier are authoritative: *Renan* (Paris, 1923); *La Pensée religieuse de Renan* (Paris, 1925); and *La Jeunesse cléricale de Renan* (Paris, 1933). The best short surveys are P. Van Tieghem, *Renan* (Paris, 1948), and M. Weiler, *La Pensée de Renan* (Grenoble, 1945).

ECLECTICS AND LIBERALS

These thinkers have been too little examined in recent decades; the best studies are mainly in French. J. M. Carré, *Michelet et son temps* (Paris, 1926), and G. Monod, *La Vie et la pensée de Michelet*, 2 vols (Paris, 1923), both remain important, and more recent studies include O. A. Haac, *Les Principes inspirateurs de Michelet* (New Haven, 1951), and J. L. Cornuz, *Jules Michelet* (Geneva and Paris, 1955). On the Eclectics there is little other than P. Dubois, *Cousin, Jouffroy, Damiron* (Paris, 1902), and P. Janet, *Victor Cousin et son œuvre*, 3rd ed. (Paris, 1893), though much useful material is contained in J. Barthélemy-Saint Hilaire, *V. Cousin, sa vie et sa correspondance*, 3 vols (Paris, 1895). On Quinet, one may consult R. H. Powers, *Edgar Quinet: A Study in French Patriotism* (Dallas, 1957), and H. Tronchon, *Le Jeune Edgar Quinet* (Paris, 1937), in particular. On Jouffroy, interesting but incomplete studies are Dubois, op. cit.; M. Salomon, *Jouffroy* (Paris, 1907); and (authoritative but on limited subjects) J. Pommier, *Deux études sur Jouffroy et son temps* (Paris, 1930).

HISTORY, PROGRESS AND POLITICAL THOUGHT

These subjects are treated less in this volume than in Professor Peyre's chapter in *French Literature from 1600 to the Present* (London, 1974), ch. 2 (with bibliography). On the many 'secular' creeds of the nineteenth century there is a select bibliography as well as a survey in D. G. Charlton, *Secular Religions in France (1815–1870)* (London, 1963), pp. 217 ff. Considerable attention has been given to the social and political thinkers of the period – more so than to its philosophers, one may think. Amongst many studies, the following are good general surveys: R. Aron, *Main Currents in Sociological Thought*, 2 vols (London, 1968–70); C. C. A. Bouglé, *Socialismes français*, 2nd ed. (Paris, 1933); J. B. Bury, *The Idea of Progress*, 2nd ed. (New York, 1955); A. Gray, *The Socialist Tradition* (London 1946); L. Halphen, *L'Histoire en France depuis cent ans* (Paris, 1914); M. Leroy *Histoire des idées sociales en France*, Vols II and III (Paris, 1950–4); J. P. Mayer,

Political Thought in France from Sieyès to Sorel, 3rd ed. (London, 1961); P. Moreau, *L'Histoire en France au XIXe siècle* (Paris, 1935); R. Pierce, *Contemporary French Political Thought* (Oxford, 1966); R. Soltau, *French Political Thought in the Nineteenth Century* (London, 1931); and J. L. Talmon, *Political Messianism: The Romantic Phase* (London, 1952) (though this may be thought a somewhat tendentious study). On individual writers there are likewise numerous works, of which one may note in particular: D. W. Brogan, *Proudhon* (London, 1934); J. Lively, *The Social and Political Thought of Alexis de Tocqueville* (Oxford, 1962); A. Pinloche, *Fourier et le socialisme* (Paris, 1933); G. Woodcock, *P. J. Proudhon* (London, 1956); *Revue internationale de philosophie*, LX (1962), fasc. 2, *Charles Fourier*; and F. E. Manuel, *The New World of Henri Saint-Simon* (Cambridge, Mass., 1956) – a particularly full study in English – to which one can add a good selection in translation and an introduction in F. M. H. Markham, *Saint-Simon: Selected Writings* (Oxford, 1952).

THE CRITICAL REACTION

This major development in later nineteenth century French thought warrants renewed examination. The principal studies remain A. Aliotta, *The Idealistic Reaction against Science* (London, 1914); G. Fonsegrive, *L'Évolution des idées dans la France contemporaine* (Paris, 1920) (concerned more with literary than philosophical writers); two important volumes by D. Parodi, *Du positivisme à l'idéalisme*, 2 vols (Paris, 1930); and an incisive, lucid thesis by L. S. Stebbing, *Pragmatism and French Voluntarism* (Cambridge, 1914). Richard Griffiths, *The Reactionary Revolution* (London, 1966), has numerous useful insights but does not seek to explore the philosophical reaction itself. On individuals the most useful studies are S. W. Floss, *Outline of the Philosophy of Cournot* (Philadelphia, 1941); J. Grenier, *La Philosophie de Jules Lequier* (Paris, 1936); and G. Milhaud, *La Philosophie de Renouvier* (Paris, 1927); but the entire movement in which 'idealism' (in its differing senses) was opposed to 'positivism' and 'scientism' requires fresh scrutiny. Two difficult but major works on its most philosophically outstanding thinker are O. Hamelin, *Le Système de Renouvier* (Paris, 1927), and R. Verneaux, *L'Idéalisme de Renouvier* (Paris, 1945).

BERGSON AND THE NEO-SPIRITUALISTS

New general surveys are needed to supplement A. Etcheverry, *L'Idéalisme français contemporain* (Paris, 1934), and A. Thibaudet, *Le Bergsonisme*, 2 vols (Paris, 1924). Very helpful studies of individuals are provided by I. W. Alexander, *Bergson* (London, 1957); J. Chevalier, *Bergson* (Paris, 1926); G. Mauchaussat, *L'Idéalisme de Lachelier* (Paris, 1961); and G. Séailles, *La Philosophie de J. Lachelier* (Paris, 1921). A. D. Lindsay, *The Philosophy of Bergson* (London, 1911), provides an earlier but still useful English assessment of its subject.

EXISTENTIALISTS

There are numerous works of which the best general examinations are P. Foulquié, *L'Existentialisme* (Paris, 1949); R. Grimsley, *Existentialist Thought* (Cardiff, 1955); and E. Mounier, *Introduction aux existentialismes* (Paris, 1947). On individuals, likewise, there are many studies; perhaps the most helpful for English readers are S. Cain, *Gabriel Marcel* (London, 1963); N. N. Greene, *J.-P. Sartre: The Existentialist Ethic* (Ann Arbor, Michigan, 1960); I. Murdoch, *Sartre* (London, 1953); A. R. Manser, *Sartre: a Philosophic Study* (London, 1966); M. Cranston, *Sartre* (London, 1962); and G. Sennari, *Simone de Beauvoir* (Paris, 1959). In addition, a vivid evocation of existentialist debates is provided by Simone de Beauvoir, *Les Mandarins* (Paris, 1954). A useful select bibliography of primary texts is given in É. Morot-Sir, *La Pensée française d'aujourd'hui* (Paris, 1971), which goes beyond the intention of this present chapter and also deals with still-emerging movements in French thought: chs. III and VI give a survey of structuralist ideas and ch. V of present-day Marxist thought in France. C. Smith, *Contemporary French Philosophy*, is basic preparatory reading for an understanding of French philosophy since 1945.

INDEX